THE
LITTLE GIANT® BOOK
OF
KIDS'
GAMES

Written & Illustrated by
Glen Vecchione

STERLING PUBLISHING COMPANY, INC.
New York

Edited by Jeanette Green
Designed by Jeff Fitschen

Library of Congress Cataloging-in-Publication Data
Available

10 9 8 7 6 5 4 3 2 1

Published by Sterling Publishing Company, Inc.
387 Park Avenue South
New York, NY 10016–8810
© 1999 Glen Vecchione
Distributed in Canada by Sterling Publishing
$^c/o$ Canadian Manda Group, One Atlantic Avenue, Suite 105
Toronto, Ontario, Canada M6K 3E7
Distributed in Great Britain and Europe by Chris Lloyd
463 Ashley Road, Parkstone, Poole, Dorset, BH14 0AX, England
Distributed in Australia by Capricorn Link (Australia) Pty Ltd.
P. O. Box 6651, Baulkham Hills, Business Centre, NSW 2153, Australia

Sterling ISBN 0-8069-6341-7

Contents

Indoor Games

Outdoor Games

Indoor & Outdoor Games

Indoor Games

Balloon Basketball

Players: 10 or more; 2 "Baskets"; referee
Materials: Chairs for all players except the referee; inflated balloons, the more the better

Set up the chairs in two rows, about 3 feet (1 m) apart, facing each other. Place two of the chairs at each end, between the rows.

Divide the players into two teams, and let each team choose a captain. Any team member may sit in any chair, but only a team's captain may pick one of two "Baskets"—actually, players who stand on the chairs at the end of the rows. These Basket players must make hoops by holding out their arms and clasping their hands. The hoops should be big enough for a balloon to pass through.

The referee tosses a balloon into the air in the middle of the rows. Each team swats at the balloon to get it in their own Basket, but no

player may get up from a chair. The Basket can bend around on the chair and try to capture the balloon, as long as he doesn't move his feet or unclasp his hands.

Each balloon batted through a Basket is worth 2 points. If the balloon goes out of bounds, the referee tosses in a fresh balloon where the other balloon went out. After a team scores, the referee starts the play going again by tossing the balloon over the middle of the row.

A score of 20 points wins the game, or play for a set period of time with the higher-scoring team declared the winners.

Balloon Slap

Players: 8 or more in two teams; referee
Materials: Balloon, coin

This is a great game for volleyball lovers who find themselves stuck indoors. Players divide into two teams and sit in rows facing one another. Make the rows close enough together

so that players on opposite sides can almost touch each other's hands.

Place a balloon between the rows. The referee flips a coin, and one player begins the game from his seat by slapping the balloon between the rows in an effort to get it over the heads of the opposing team. If he's successful, he scores a point for his team.

The opposing team's players will, of course, try to slap the balloon back and over the heads of their competitors. But at no time may a player rise from his seat. If this happens, the referee stops the game and penalizes the offending player's team by awarding an extra point to the opposition. Then the referee places the balloon in the middle again and the team with an extra point begins another round.

If you have lots of players, you can vary this game by breaking up each team into two rows of players, one row behind the other. A balloon that falls between the rows (not over them) scores a point. This avoids having players of a team slap the ball as hard as they can without really aiming. With the two-row arrangment, a balloon that goes over both rows is declared out of bounds by the referee.

The first team to collect 15 points wins the game.

Blow Against

Players: 2; referee
Materials: Ping-Pong ball, tablespoon,
    2 books, and small electric fan for each player

If you don't have a store-bought fan to use for
this game, make a fan by accordion-folding a
piece of construction paper, or by gluing a large
paper plate to a wooden paint stirrer.

Mark out imaginary boundary lines by placing books at opposite sides of the room. Behind each boundary line, place the fan so that it tilts toward the floor.

Each player crouches beside a book, facing the other player. Each takes a spoon and holds it like a shovel close to the floor. The referee puts a Ping-Pong ball directly in front of each player's spoon, then turns on each of the fans.

Each player must push, with the spoon, his Ping-Pong ball across the floor toward the opposite player's boundary line. Of course, this gets harder the closer you get the fan! Players may stand, crawl, or crouch as they push the balls across the room, but at no time may a player touch a ball. The referee watches closely for this and sends any player who breaks the rule back to the beginning. If a Ping-Pong ball blows out of the spoon and races backwards, a player can rescue it using his spoon only.

The first player to cross his opponent's boundary line wins the race.

Blow Hard

Players: 4 or more

Materials: Chairs and straws for each
  player, a small downy feather

Players arrange their chairs in a circle and sit
close together facing the inside of the circle.
One player stands and tosses the feather in the
air above the center of the circle. Then each
player, without standing, blows through the
straw to keep the feather from floating down. If
the feather touches a player, that player leaves
the game and the circle of chairs grows smaller. The feather is tossed in the air again, and
the game continues as before.

Players must never leave their chairs while
blowing the feather, but any player may choose
not to use the straw if she chooses. This is usually a good idea if the feather comes very close
to someone's face. Besides protecting herself

from the falling feather, a player can also try to blow her feather toward another player to take him out.

If the feather falls to the floor without touching anyone, the original feather-tosser starts the game over. The winner of the game is the sole remaining player.

Bubble Hoops

Players: 2 or more
Materials: Soap bubbles, 7 feet (2.3 m) of
   wire, 14 sewing spools, Post-it notes, marker,
   long table

This game requires a little preparation. Cut the
wire into seven 1-foot (30 cm) sections, and bend
each section into a hoop. Stick the ends of each
hoop into the spools, and place the hoops on a
table top, following the diagram. Hoops should
be about 2 feet (60 cm) from each other, a little
farther if your table is large enough. To show the
playing order of the hoops, mark the numbers
1–9 on Post-it notes, and fold each note around
the top of each hoop. Notice how the starting
hoop (1) is also the finishing hoop (9).

   The first player blows a soap bubble and fans
it through the first hoop. If the bubble makes it
through without breaking, he blows another

bubble and fans it through the second hoop. Or, if he's lucky enough to get his bubble through both hoops without it breaking, he just keeps going. Play continues until the player's bubble breaks. Then it's the second player's turn.

The first player to get through the sequence of numbered hoops wins the game.

Bubble-Pong

Players: 2 to 4 players in teams

Materials: Soap bubbles for each player or team; construction paper; Ping-Pong table (or table plus 2 pencils, clay, colored yarn, construction paper)

Except for the soap bubbles and construction paper, you can forget the rest of the materials if you have a Ping-Pong table. If not, find the middle of a table and place two balls of clay at the edges. Stick pencils into the balls of clay so that the pencils stand upright like posts. Stretch a long piece of brightly colored yarn across the pencils for a "dividing net." Fold the construction paper accordionlike into fans, one for each player.

The first player begins by blowing a soap bubble and then fanning it across the net to her opponent. This player, in turn, tries to fan the

bubble back across the net. If a player gets the bubble to burst on his opponent's side of the table, he gets a point and blows the next bubble.

A player may not lean across the net while fanning the bubble to the other side. If this happens, the opponent may call "Foul!" and the offending player loses a point. It might help to have a referee observe the game if this is a serious competition.

The first player to reach a score of 21 points wins Bubble-Pong.

Clumps

Players: 10 or more, an even number

Materials: Any small object in the room that
  can be carried

Players form two circles, each circle standing
about 10 feet (3 m) from the other. One member of each circle goes out to select some small
item to bring back into the circle. The item can

be a book, a vase, a piece of fruit, a small bowl, or anything that can be easily hidden from the players of the opposing circle.

A player in the first circle calls out a question about the hidden item to a player in the second circle. The question might be "Is the object heavy?" or "Does the object have any moving parts?" The player can only answer with a "yes" or "no." Now the answering player calls out a question to a player in the first circle. Again, this player must answer only "yes" or "no."

Questions and answers go back and forth between all the players in the circles, and every player in each circle should get a chance to either question or answer. The first circle to guess the object hidden by the other circle takes one of the losing circle's players. Now the game starts over, this time with one circle larger than the other.

A circle goes out of the game when it loses one of its two remaining players. As a variation, and if you have enough players, you can make three circles instead of two.

Creeping Cats

Players: 6 or more
Materials: 2 books to mark safe zone
Surface: Carpeted

Place two books about 10 feet (3 m) apart and imagine a line stretching between them. This is the safe zone.

All players get down on their hands and knees. The Cats start out behind the safe zone while the Dogs wait for them on the opposite side of the room, facing away. Choose one play-

er to be the Top Dog. This Dog will listen for the approach of the Cats and tell the other Dogs when to turn and chase them.

At the start signal, the Cats creep slowly toward the Dogs while the Top Dog listens for their approach. Since the Dogs can't see them, the Cats must be very quiet and sneaky. Any Cat lucky enough get close enough to a Dog may tag him and take him out of the game. Of course, when this happens, all the Dogs know the Cats have arrived and so turn and crawl after them as they scurry for the safe zone. Any Cat tagged by a Dog goes out of the game as well.

But what usually happens is that a Cat or two comes very close before the Top Dog hears her and yells "Cats!" That's when all the Dogs turn and give chase.

The Dogs win if they can chase the Cats, tag them, and take them all out of the game. The Cats win if they can take the Dogs out of the game by sneaking up and tagging them. It's usually a pretty close match!

Flour Tower

Players: 2
Materials: Flour, shallow bowl, cutting
   board, coin, plastic knives, table

This game can get messy, so set it up on a table with a moist sponge nearby. Still, it is best to play it indoors because of possible wind problems outdoors.

Fill the bowl with flour and press the flour tightly down, compacting it. Place the cutting board over the bowl and then turn both board and bowl over so that the bowl rests upside-down. Carefully lift the bowl so that you have a mound of compacted flour.

Place a coin in the center of the mound, and give each player a plastic knife. Players take turns slicing away the flour, one turn each. At first, it's easy. But as more and more flour slices away, the coin has less to hold it up. Eventually, only a slender tower of flour holds the coin up, and each player has to slide pretty carefully.

The player who topples the coin loses.

Globe Spinners

Players: 4 or more in pairs

Materials: Spinning globe; atlas; clock with second hand; blindfold; pencil and notepad for each team

In this geography game, each team keeps track of the competing team's progress. Players sit around a small table with their pads and pencils. At the center of the table, place a globe. Keep the clock and atlas on the table, too.

The first player in Team #1 stands. The second player spins the globe as fast as possible. Then the first player, without looking, stops the spinning globe with his finger. He calls out the place where his finger stopped, and his teammate must list everything he knows about the place in 15 seconds. If the country is Australia for example, he might write "kangaroos, Sydney, Crocodile Dundee,

Ayre's Rock, Southern Hemisphere, down under . . ." while the other team watches the clock and calls "Time!" when 15 seconds are up.

Team #1 reads its list to Team #2 who records the number of items. If Team #2 challenges any item on the list as incorrect, the atlas is used, and either the listing team or challenging team lose a turn. The game continues as teams take turns spinning and timing.

Of course, stopping the globe with your finger doesn't always mean landing on a country. If a spinner lands in the ocean, his teammate has 15 seconds to list everything she can peculiar to that ocean. If it's the Atlantic Ocean, for instance, she might list "Plymouth Rock, Maine, whaling ships, and Boston Harbor." If it's the Mediterranean, she'll have to think about the French Riviera and ancient Greece.

The first team to reach 100 points wins the game.

Huckle, Buckle, Beanstalk

Players: 3 or more
Materials: Chair

This game sharpens your observation skills and makes you a good detective. You'll be amazed at how long it'll take some of your friends to catch on.

The game should take place in a room familiar to all the players. Place a chair in the center of the room, and choose someone to be "IT" from among the players. IT sends the other players out. He then selects some small object in the room—a book, a vase, a plant, a picture—and moves it to some outlandish place where it doesn't belong but won't be too conspicuous.

IT calls the other players back in, and each player looks for something different about the

room. When a player notices the object, he shouts "Huckle, buckle, beanstalk!" and races to the chair. Sometimes, two or more players recognize the object at about the same time. They all call "Huckle, buckle, beanstalk!" but only one will make it to the chair.

The player sitting in the chair first becomes IT for the next game.

Hunters & Hounds

Players: 8 or more in two teams; referee
Materials: 20 dog biscuits, 2 paper bags

In preparation for the game, the referee goes around the house and hides 20 dog biscuits in various locations.

Each team chooses a Hunter. The rest of the players on the team become Hounds. Both teams start in the same room of the house, and the Hounds practice barking and howling for their Hunter so that he can learn to recognize their sounds.

At a signal from the referee, the Hounds of each team dash around the house looking for dog biscuits while the Hunters stay behind holding their paper bags. When a Hound from either team finds a biscuit, he doesn't pick it up, but signals the hunter to come get it by barking and howling. Hunters should listen

closely in order to recognize the sounds of their Hounds. When a Hunter hears one of his Hounds, he follows the sound to the dog biscuit, picks it up, and places it in the bag. Then he listens for more of his Hounds and follows the sound.

Sometimes Hounds of rival teams reach a dog biscuit at the same time. In this case *both* Hunters, assuming each recognizes his Hounds through the noise of his opponent's Hounds, rush to the scene to pick up the bone. Of course, only one gets there first!

The referee should keep count of all the bones in the Hunters' bags and call out how many bones remain undiscovered. When the last bone is picked up, the referee takes a last count, and the Hunter with the greater number of bones wins the game for his team.

Mystery Adverb

Players: 4 or more
Materials: None

This game combines charades with word guessing. Send one player out of the room. The remaining players choose between them the mystery adverb, preferring one that can be easily demonstrated. Good choices are adverbs like *angrily, sleepily, happily, quickly, strangely,* or *hysterically*.

Call the player in again and tell him that he has to discover the mystery adverb by asking any of the others to act it out in some way. For example, he might ask one of the players to walk across the room. Another has to make a speech. He asks another to shake hands or sing a song—the variations are endless.

Players try to both give clues and confuse

the guesser. When he finally discovers the mystery adverb, another player leaves the room and the game starts all over again.

Peanut Pitch

Players: 2 or more

Materials: 5 unshelled peanuts for each
   player, 3 bowls of different sizes that
   you can nest

Place the smallest bowl into the next smallest, and place both of those bowls into the larger bowl. Fill the center bowl with water, but pour just a little water into the surrounding bowls. If any of the bowls float, add more water to the center bowl and remove water from the surrounding bowls.

Each player takes his five peanuts and stands 6 feet (2 m) from the bowl. He tosses his peanuts toward the bowl. A peanut that lands in the outside bowl counts 2 points, 4 points if it lands in the inner bowl, and 10 points if it lands in the center bowl. A peanut that misses the bowl counts no points.

After a player finishes pitching his peanuts, he removes them from the bowl (where they float) and counts up his points. Then it's the next player's turn. The first player to reach 100 points wins the game.

Phantom Hands

Players: 2 or more; Lamp Keeper
Materials: Hooded desk lamp

More of a trick than a game, Phantom Hands will still amuse your friends, if not spook them out of their wits. It's a great stunt for a Halloween Party.

This trick works by fooling the eyes into seeing something that isn't really there through the effect of *retinal afterimage*. You've probably already experienced something like it when a flashbulb popped in your face.

Choose one player to be the Lamp Keeper. The lamp itself should be of the metal-hooded variety, easily switched on and off, and with a good strong light that the Lamp Keeper can direct downward.

For the trick to work, you'll need to darken the room completely; so choose a place in the

room near a light switch. Players sit in a tight circle on the floor. Each player places one hand in the center of the circle so that the hands pile up. The Lamp Keeper places the lamp directly over the hands without blocking any player's view of the hands.

When everyone sits comfortably, the Lamp Keeper gets up and switches off the room light.

He instructs everyone to sit quietly and keep their hands very still. The silent sitting continues for at least 2 minutes so that players' eyes adjust to the darkness.

The Lamp Keeper then instructs the players to look down in the general direction of the piled hands. He flashes the light for no more than a second, revealing the hands. He then tells the players to slowly remove their hands from the circle but to *keep their eyes fixed* to where they saw the hands.

If these instruction have been followed carefully, each player will "see" a perfect photographic image of the pile of hands appearing before him in the darkness. The image will be a ghostly blue or pink. Invite the players to carefully move their real hands to touch the phantom hands. Creepy!

Poisoned Pincushions

Players: 10 or more
Materials: 3 or 4 big pillows or cushions

Except for IT, players stand in a circle holding hands and facing inward. IT stands at the center of the circle next to the "poisoned pincush-

ions." At the start signal, IT walks to one of the circle players and attempts to drag him to the center and toss him on one of the poisoned cushions. The players on either side of the dragged player may hold on, but they can't step out of the circle or break hands with the players next to them. If IT succeeds in dragging the player to a poisoned cushion, the poisoned player dies and goes out of the game.

The circle of players tightens as each player gets poisoned. Finally, only IT and a single player are left. The game ends with the single player and IT struggling to drag each other to the poisoned cushion. The winner is the sole remaining player.

Racing Colors

Players: 10 or more in two teams; referee

Materials: Construction paper, pack with many colors; fruits and vegetables in many colors, such as yellow banana, red apple, purple grapes, orange, green lettuce, and brown potato. Substitute a crumpled ball of construction paper for any color for which you can't obtain a fruit or vegetable.

In this relay game, the racers have to step across a path made of different colors of sheets of construction paper, but they can only step on the color called by the referee.

Each team prepares the construction paper path for the other team. Divide the pack of construction paper so that each team has an equal number of sheets and colors. The paths should be about 10 yards (9 m) long, and the colors should mix evenly so that it's possible to walk along the path on any one color without jumping too far. It doesn't matter which end of the path you choose for starting, but both teams should agree.

Divide your team in half so that the same number of players stand at opposite ends of the path. Lay out an equal number of fruits and vegetables on opposite ends, too. The first player of each team stands beside the fruits and vegetables. His teammates line up behind him and stand in a line at the opposite end of the path.

The referee begins the game by calling "1, 2, 3 . . ." and then a color. For example, if the referee calls out "Yellow!" the first players must pick up the bananas and then step only on yellow sheets of construction paper as they walk across. When they reach the opposite end, players hand their bananas to the next player in the relay line. However, if the referee calls out "Red!" the next players must put down their bananas and grab the apples before stepping on only red squares. Of course, the referee may choose to call "Yellow!" again, in which case the next in line keeps the banana.

As the race continues, the referee watches to make sure that the players pick up the correct fruit and step only on the named color. Any racer who gets "color confused" must go back to the beginning of the path. This is also true for any racer who stumbles off a color.

The first team to completely switch sides wins the game.

Road Map

Players: 3 or more; referee

Materials: Blindfold for each player, large fold-out road map of your area, tape measure, red crayon, construction paper, cellophane tape, and any small articles of furniture that can be used to make an obstacle course

On the road map, find your location—whether city or street—as precisely as you can, and make a big X over it with the red crayon. Tape the map to the wall. Cut out little car shapes from the construction paper, one for each player. Attach a small piece of cellophane tape to each car shape. As a final preparation, arrange the small pieces of furniture so that the players will have an obstacle course to get through as they cross the room toward the map.

Standing on the opposite side of the room from the map, the players have one minute to study the obstacle course before all the players are blindfolded and the first player is handed a paper car by the referee. The referee spins this player around three times and sends her on her way.

The player holds the car in front of her and, trying to remember where the obstacles lie, carefully crosses the room to the map. The referee should stand beside the crossing player to make sure she doesn't trip across something and fall, but the first bump against an obstacle counts as a point against her, the second bump counts again, and a third bump takes her out of the game.

If she manages to cross to the road map, she must now pin her car to the map. The object is to pin the car as far from the X as possible without going off the map.

The next player repeats the routine, and then the next player, until all players have either reached the road map and attached their cars, or they have been disqualified by bumping and being taken out of the game.

Now all players remove their blindfolds. The referee goes to the map and uses the tape measure to see which car is farthest from the crayoned X. Any player who has pinned his car on the bare wall is disqualified. The player farthest from the X wins the game.

Scissor Legs

Players: 8 or more
Materials: Small rubber ball
Surface: Smooth floor

This game resembles a human pinball machine. Each team tries to stop a rolling ball from scoring points by using scissor legs to block it.

Teams sit on the floor opposite each other at a distance of around 20 feet (6 m). If you have enough players, stretch them from wall to wall so that the rolling ball can't go around the players, only through them. Players of a team sit about 3 feet (1 m) apart with their legs stretched straight out and close together.

The spaces between players count for points. Moving from left to right, the space between the first and second players counts 3 points; the space between the second and third player counts 5 points, and so on, in incre-

ments of two, until you reach the last player.

Teams toss a coin to see who will be first. The starting team's player begins the game by rolling the ball toward the opposing team. He wants to get the ball through a particular space between players for points. But when those two players see the ball coming, they open their legs, closing the spaces between them. Then one of them grabs the stopped ball and rolls it back again. Now the rolling team must close up its spaces.

The ball goes back and forth quickly, and players must really pay attention. When a team scores points, it starts the ball again for the next round. The first team to reach 50 points wins the game.

Slip the Bean

Players: 5 or more
Materials: 10 dried beans for each player

Play this game in a room where nobody can escape. Give each player 10 beans, one of which will always stay hidden in the palm of the hand. Tell the players that they all have to get acquainted by shaking hands, and when a player shakes hands with the tenth person, he slips that player his bean. And he continues to shake hands to get rid of the other nine beans. The point of the game is to get rid of all your beans before anyone else does.

This handshaking can get pretty hilarious, with everyone slipping the bean to everyone else while, at the same time, having beans slipped to them. You have to be sneaky by not letting the tenth player know that you're about to slip him the bean; otherwise, he'll avoid you. Of course, no player can refuse a bean either.

The first player to get rid of all his beans declares himself the winner.

Storm Watch

Players: 5 or more
Materials: None

Depending on the size of the room, any number of players can enjoy this game. Name the four sides of the room after the four points of the compass, North, South, East, and West. Players—the Weathervanes—choose a side and stand there. One player is the Wind and stands in the center of the room.

The game begins when the Wind points to one side of the room, calls out a direction, and all of the Weathervanes immediately face the opposite direction. For example, if the Wind calls "North!" the Weathervanes must face South. If she shouts "East!" the Weathervanes all turn West. If she shouts "Variable!" the Weathervanes stand on their toes and sway back and forth. And finally, if the Wind shouts

"Storm!" all Weathervanes must spin around three times and stop.

Of course, these directions come fast and furiously, and any player who slips up and disobeys a command from the Wind goes out of the game. The last remaining player wins.

Strange Silhouettes

Players: 5 or more

Materials: Large white sheet; gooseneck
  desk lamp or similar lamp; small table; costume articles, such as hats, wigs, scarves,
  and false noses

In this version of Blind Man's Buff, the chosen
player has to recognize his friends by their silhouettes.

Tack the large white sheet to an open door-
way so that you cover most of the opening.
Place the small table about 6 feet (2 m) from
the sheet, and place the lamp on top of the
table. Turn the lamp so that the light shines
directly on the sheet.

The chosen player sits on the side of the
sheet opposite the lamp. The remaining players prepare for the game by putting on various
costume articles. One player switches on the

lamp, and then each player parades between the sheet and the lamp so that his silhouette appears on the opposite side of the sheet. Besides wearing costumes, players can also crouch down to disguise their real heights—but no talking is allowed.

The chosen player tries to recognize each of his friends by their strange silhouettes alone. Players can give the chosen player more time by pausing in front of the sheet and doing some little piece of business. But remember, if the chosen player recognizes you, you have to change places with him.

Stuff the Turkey

Players: 4 or more in pairs; referee
Materials: 10 inflated balloons for each
team, laundry basket for each team, T-shirt
for one player in each team
Surface: Soft surface

Stuff the Turkey is hilarious, if not a little
noisy. Prepare for the game by blowing up 10
balloons for each pair of players. Place these
balloons in the laundry baskets. One player of
each pair also gets a T-shirt to wear.

At the start signal from the referee, Player
#1 of each team reaches into the laundry bas-
ket, pulls out a balloon, and hands it to Player
#2. Player #2 "stuffs the turkey"—that is, he
squeezes the balloon under his T-shirt, then
rolls around the floor trying to burst the balloon under his weight. When he succeeds, he
stands up for another balloon.

This is a hilarious spectacle, with players rolling and popping balloons all over the place. It's also a great game to watch, so call in all your friends.

The first pair of players to pop all their balloons can declare themselves the winners.

This or That?

Players: 3 or more
Materials: None

This ESP (extrasensory perception) game will have your friends puzzled and perplexed, but you'll need a secret partner to share the trick of the game. This is how it works: Gather your friends together for a demonstration of mind-reading. Choose one person (your secret partner) to leave the room. Ask any one of the others to choose an object in the room that you'll communicate telepathically. After the object is chosen, call your partner back in the room.

Now for the demonstration. Point to any of the unchosen objects in the room and ask your partner, "Is it this?" She'll answer no. In fact, she'll answer "No" to anything you point out unless you ask her "Is it *that*?" By using the word *that* instead of *this*, you secretly identify the correct object to your partner.

One way to really impress the others is to continue for some time asking your partner "Is it this?" so that the others get used to the question. Then allow someone else in the room to ask a question or two. Chances are, they'll continue to point out incorrect objects with the question "Is it this?" Then you can take back the questioning and continue as before.

Under the Table

Players: 5 or more; Leader

Materials: Large table, large wastepaper
basket, cardboard box, clock or watch with a
second hand, chair for each player, pencil
and pad for each player, and an assortment
of small, unbreakable objects the Leader
chooses and hides from other players

Before starting, the Leader makes a list of all
the objects she intends to pass under the table.
She'll use this list to score the players at the
end of the game. Some good choices for objects
are fruits, a key, a cork, a ball, a spoon—and
even some odd things like a corkscrew or mag-
nifying glass. The Leader keeps these objects
hidden in a cardboard box.

Players sit at the table with their hands
underneath. A big wastepaper basket sits at one

end of the table. The Leader sits at the opposite end and passes the first object to the player seated next to her. This player passes the object to the next player, and so on, until the last player drops the object into the wastepaper basket.

Each player can take only an instant to feel each object because the Leader continues to pass objects rapidly and no two objects may pile up.

When the Leader passes the last object, she calls "Finish!" Players then have 30 seconds to write down all the objects they recognized. The Leader compares each player's list with her complete list. A player gets a point for each object accurately identified. The player with the highest score wins the game.

Up, Jenkins!

Players: 6 or more in two teams
Materials: Large coin, square table, chair
   for each player

Divide the players into two teams, each team
sitting at opposite sides of the table. Both
teams choose a Captain, who gives the commands for his team.

One team starts with a coin—preferably a
large coin—that team members pass back and
forth under the table. When the opposing
Captain calls "Up, Jenkins!" the team with the
coin must clench their hands and raise them
above the table so that all hands are visible to
the opposing team. Of course, the coin is hidden in one of these hands, and it's the job of the
opposing team's Captain to find it.

When the Captain calls "Down, Jenkins!"
players must slap their hands flat against the

tabletop, and the player with the coin has to hide or disguise the sound of the coin hitting the table. Her teammates may help by slapping their hands down loudly, or bumping the underside of the table with a knee, but no shouting is allowed.

Now the Captain, by consulting his teammates, must discover which hand covers the coin. One by one, he asks players to raise their hands. For every wrong hand he chooses, the coin team gets a point. If he chooses the correct hand the first time, he gets a bonus of 5 points for his team.

Sides reverse, with the coin team now calling "Up, Jenkins!" The first team to reach 25 points wins the game.

Outdoor Games

Aliens

Players: 6 to 12

Materials: None

Surface: Paved or grassy; a large area, like several backyards, with plenty of hiding places

If the thought of UFOs and creatures from outer space sends shivers up your spine, this is the game for you! It's particularly creepy to play at night, with just a few lampposts or porch lights for illumination.

Mark out two dens—a Starting Den and a Safety Den. The dens should be far apart and out of sight of each other. Assemble everyone inside the Starting Den and choose one player to be the Alien. While the rest of the players cover their eyes and count to 100, the Alien goes off to hide somewhere between the two dens. After the count is finished, one of the waiting players calls out: "Flying saucer! It landed in the woods!" This warns the Alien to keep low and still.

Now, one at a time, players leave the Starting Den and try to cross over to the Safety Den. Of course, to do this, they must pass through the area where the saucer landed and

the Alien is lurking. If the Alien jumps out of hiding and tags a crossing player, that player becomes an Alien, too. Now both hide and wait for the next player to cross. If, on the other hand, the crossing player outruns the Alien and reaches the Safety Den, or if he never encounters the Alien *at all* during his crossing, he waits in the Safety Den for the next player to join him.

Players may choose to either run or walk across; but if the dens are very far apart, each player should wait about a minute before following the player ahead of him. Another strategy is to sneak across, keeping out of sight of the Alien as you creep to the other side. But if you plan to cross this way, let the next player know so he'll give you a few extra minutes.

This is the eeriest part of the game. As each player disappears into the darkness ahead, you don't know whether any of them ever reach the Safety Den.

Players in the Safety Den have an important job to do now. As each player in the Starting Den begins to cross, he may choose to signal the Safe Players to find out how many (if any) have made it across to the Safety Den. If all the Safe Players made it across, there's only one Alien out there, and he may decide to slowly and carefully sneak across. If none of them have, and a small army of Aliens is waiting for him, he may have to change his strategy—maybe by running from one hiding place to the next!

At some point, there may be more Aliens than players waiting to cross. If so, the Aliens may creep up on the players in the Starting Den and then leap out at them for a final chase. Any player tagged before reaching the Safety Den becomes an Alien. Now every player is either safe or an Alien. Whichever side has the most players wins the game.

All Sewn Up

Players: 10 to 20
Materials: None
Surface: Paved or grassy

This unusual chase game has a mathematical twist. Players stand in a circle, leaving enough space between each player for another player to pass through. Two players, let's say Eric and Joan, stand in the center.

On the word "Go!" Eric and Joan separate and run between the standing players, weaving in and out of the circle. Each time either one passes between two standing players, the players link hands and close up the space, so the circle is gradually "sewn up."

Eric's goal is to sew up the circle and capture Joan inside. He must calculate his moves carefully though, or he may sew himself up, too! Or, he may find to his dismay, that she's outside and he's inside! Joan has the same plan. Both players must watch carefully and try to keep just one step ahead of each other—that's what makes this game so challenging.

Should both players be sewn up together, they must repeat the game until one is captured. The captured player joins the circle and chooses a replacement.

Around the World

Players: 2 to 5
Materials: Basketball, tape
Surface: Basketball court

Tape seven evenly spaced X's to the floor in a semicircular pattern around the basketball hoop, none closer than 20 feet (6 m). Player #1

shoots from the first X. If the ball goes through, he moves to the second X, and so on, until he misses. When he misses, he loses his turn, and Player #2 begins on the first X.

When Player #1's turn comes up again, he continues shooting from the X where he left off and continues "around the world" until he misses a shot. Player #2 then shoots from where he left off, and the game proceeds until one player has moved across all seven X's and back again.

Balloon-Face Relay

Players: 16 to 40, an even number, in
two teams

Materials: 2 large balloons, partially inflated;
chalk or rope for marking starting and finish
lines

Surface: Paved or grassy

It's a good idea to have the pairs of racers on
each team matched for height, since that's part
of an effective winning strategy for this game.

Inflate two balloons so that each one is firm
enough to hold its shape but soft enough to be
carried between two faces—that's right, two
faces. Using chalk or rope, mark starting and
finish lines at opposite sides of the racing field,
about 15 yards (4.5 m) apart.

Each racer pairs off with another member
of his own team, and each team divides in half,

so that half of the pairs of racers wait behind the starting line, opposite the other half behind the finish line.

At the starting line, one player of each pair holds a balloon at his side and waits for the "Go!" signal. At the signal, he squeezes the balloon between his face and that of his partner's, and both clasp their hands behind their backs. Then both partners start walking as fast as possible toward the finish line. Only a sideways walk is possible, and hands must remain clasped behind backs while the balloon is carried. If the balloon slips out from between the two faces, it must hit the ground before either player may unclasp his hands and pick it up.

Since that usually takes enough time to slow down a pair of racers considerably, the pair does *not* have to return to the starting line as a penalty.

When the first pair of racers reaches the finish line, they must cross it completely before transferring the balloon to the second pair of waiting racers. No hands can be used in the switch! The second pair approaches the balloon perpendicularly from opposite sides, and maneuvers around so that the balloon is switched without being dropped.

The second pair of racers walks back to the starting line where the third pair waits, and so on. When the last pair comes back from the finish line side, they win the game for their team.

Bounce-Off Bowling

Players: 2 to 6

Materials: Medium-size inflated ball (or soccerball, basketball, etc.); 10 large plastic soda-pop bottles; chalk or rope

Surface: Flat paved or grassy, with nearby wall

You can either bowl or toss the ball in this knock-'em-down game. Try to find a flat surface and sturdy wall for the ricochet shots.

At a distance of 10 feet (3 m) in front of the wall, arrange the soda-pop bottles in a circle 8 feet (2.4 m) in diameter. Make sure you separate the bottles just enough for the ball to pass through the circle. Using chalk or rope, mark a starting line for players, 10 feet (3 m) long and 20 feet (6 m) from the edge of the circle.

Players, in turn, stand behind the starting line. A player may stand either at the middle of the starting line or at one of the ends, depending upon the direction in which he chooses to bowl his ball. For instance, a ball may either pass through the circle before hitting the wall or roll beside the circle before hitting the wall, but only the bottles knocked down *after* the ball ricochets off the wall count for points. Bottles knocked over before the ball hits the wall count against you.

Each player takes three turns, knocking over as many bottles as possible for points. After three turns, total the score and set the bottles up again. The next player begins a new round.

For a more forceful and vigorous bowling game, you can weigh down the plastic bottles by pouring a little sand or water in each one.

The first player to reach a score of 21 wins the game.

Box Baseball

Players: 2
Materials: Rubber ball, chalk (optional)
Surface: Paved

Box Baseball is played across three sidewalk squares—one for each "team" (player) and a third for the strike area. It should look like this:

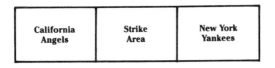

Player #1 is the California Angels, and Player #2 is the New York Yankees. Or make one the Vancouver Bears and the other the Aussie Joeys, or whatever you choose. Player #1 throws the ball into Player #2's box, passing it over the strike area. Player #2, standing outside his box, tries to catch the ball after one bounce. If he succeeds, it counts as an out for the Angels.

But if he doesn't catch the ball after one bounce, each additional bounce means one more base for the Angels. Here's what additional bounces mean:

2 bounces—**a single**
3 bounces—**a double**
4 bounces—**a triple**
5 bounces—**a home run**

If Player #1's throw bounces into the strike area, or it misses Player #2's box, that's **strike one,** and he must throw again. As in ordinary baseball, three strikes make an **out,** and it's Player #2's turn to throw.

After nine innings, the team with the higher score wins.

Buzzzz

Players: 10 to 20, an even number
Materials: Chalk or rope
Surface: Paved or grassy

Divide the players into two teams and draw a long line separating them. Team #1 sends a player into Team #2 territory, and he tags as many Team #2 players as he can. While he is tagging them, he must make the sound "Buzzzz" in one long continuous breath—loud enough for everyone to hear. If the tagger can make it back across the line to his own team without running out of breath, the players he

tagged are out of the game. But if Team #2 holds him long enough—by grabbing his arms or legs or pinning him to the ground—he runs out of breath and is eliminated himself.

Teams take turns sending a player into enemy territory. The first team to annihilate the other wins.

Cat & Mouse

Players: 10 to 20
Materials: None
Surface: Paved or grassy

This game has also been called Thread the Needle, and after trying it, you'll see why. One player is the Mouse. The other players form a circle, linking hands and holding them up high enough for Cat and Mouse to pass under.

Mouse walks around the outside of the circle. Then suddenly it tags one of the others and rushes away. The player tagged becomes the Cat and must chase Mouse as it weaves in and out of the circle, under the arms of the other players. Cat must follow Mouse's moves exactly and cannot take shortcuts across the circle.

If Mouse is caught, it joins the others in the circle and Cat becomes the new Mouse.

Chicken Fight

Players: 4 to 10, an even number
Materials: None
Surface: Grassy

For this game, players pair up, and the smaller player climbs onto the shoulders of the larger one. Together, they are "the Chicken." Several Chickens prepare for battle by strutting around, looking ferocious.

Suddenly, one Chicken charges another. The players underneath do the running and backing away, while the top players push and pull each other. The object is to knock a top player off the shoulders of his partner.

If you're playing with more than two Chickens, you may want to fight two at a time, and then re-match the winners. Or you can enjoy a free-for-all Chicken Fight!

Chinese Handball

Players: 5
Materials: Ball, chalk
Surface: Paved; wall behind playing area

Divide the space directly in front of the wall into five sections, each one about 4 feet (1.2 m) square. Or, divide the pavement into squares and let each player take a square.

Players stand back about 5 feet (1.5 m) from their squares. The player in Square #1 begins the game by slamming the ball against the ground in his own square so that it bounces up,

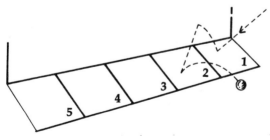

ricochets against the wall, and bounces into another player's square. That player must catch the ball and toss it back the same way—throwing it against the ground in his own square with enough force to make it rebound against the wall and fall into some other player's square. And so it goes, each player hitting the ball back in the same way. When the game gets going, there's plenty of running around. Players don't usually stay close to their own squares for long as they angle for position.

Players who miss a catch, or who throw the ball without bouncing it first, are eliminated from the game, and the remaining players move one square to the right. The last remaining player is the winner.

Kings

Kings, a variation on Chinese Handball, is played for points. Player #1 stands behind the first square and throws the ball into Player #2's square, hitting the sidewalk first and then the wall. Player #3 throws the ball the same way to Player #4, who throws it to Player #5, who returns it to Player #4, and so on. Any player who fumbles a throw or a catch receives 1 count against him. At 11 counts, he is taken out of the game, and the remaining players move one square to the right. The player who eliminates all the others and winds up in the first square is called the King.

Chinese Tag

Players: 5 to 10
Materials: None
Surface: Paved or grassy

Nobody knows how this tag game got its name, but don't let that stop you from trying it.

Whenever IT tags a player, that player not

only becomes IT, but he must also place his hand over the part of his body that was tagged. So if Nancy was tagged on the shoulder, she places a hand on her shoulder, and she has to tag someone else without using that hand. If she manages to tag John on the knee, she is no longer IT and can remove her hand from her shoulder. Now, John—hand on knee—hobbles after her and anyone else nearby. IT may use only his free hand to tag another player, but depending on where the other hand is placed, he may find it difficult to get around. Try chasing someone with your hand stuck to your toe!

Closet Dodge Ball

Players: 6

Materials: Chalk, small rubber ball

Surface: Paved; high wall

You can play this scaled-down version of Dodge Ball with six people, a wall, and a smaller ball than that used for Dodge Ball. Five players stand against the wall, about 5 feet (1.5 m) apart, separated by chalk lines drawn up the wall, the "closets." The sixth player, who stands

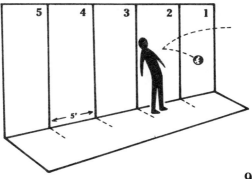

about 30 feet (9 m) away, throws the ball at any one of them. A player may twist and duck out of the way, but he may not leave his closet. If he's hit, it's 1 count against him. After 3 counts, he's out of the game. If a player catches the ball, he changes places with the thrower, who has to take on all the counts against him as well. The last remaining player wins.

Coin Pitching

Players: 3 to 6
Materials: 5 coins for each player
Surface: Paved, facing wall

Player #1 throws a coin against the curb or the lower part of a wall. Player #2 pitches one in the same way. If it lands within a handspan (from the tip of the thumb to the tip of the small finger) of Players #1's coin, Player #2 may claim it. If Player #2's coin is further away than a handspan, Player #3 follows, trying to throw his coin so that he may claim one or both of the coins that are out there. There's no limit to the number of coins you can collect if your coin falls a handspan away.

Continue the game until one player has all the loot.

Crab Race

Players: 3 to 10
Materials: 2 ropes, each about 6 feet (1.8 m)
Surface: Grassy

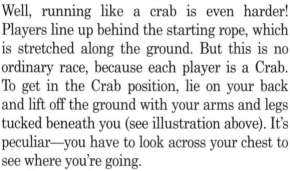

Do you know how hard it is to walk like a crab? Well, running like a crab is even harder! Players line up behind the starting rope, which is stretched along the ground. But this is no ordinary race, because each player is a Crab. To get in the Crab position, lie on your back and lift off the ground with your arms and legs tucked beneath you (see illustration above). It's peculiar—you have to look across your chest to see where you're going.

Choose a player to be the referee. He gives the "Go!" signal and stands at the finish line as the crabs race by—a hysterical sight!

Duck, Duck, Goose

Players: 10 to 20
Materials: None
Surface: Paved or grassy

This game keeps you alert! The players sit in a circle facing in. IT walks around the outside of the circle, stopping here and there to tap a sitting player and say, "Duck." This often goes on for a while as IT waits for his friends to relax so he can catch them off guard.

Suddenly IT taps a player, yells "Goose!" and rushes away. The tagged player must leap up and race around the circle in the opposite direction to reclaim his space. That is, unless IT gets there first!

The player left without a space in the circle becomes IT in the next round.

Haley-Over

Players: 9 to 17 in two teams; referee
Materials: Softball
Surface & Place: Paved or grassy; a wall
   or small building high enough to hide the
   teams from each other

An exciting sport that has come down to us from colonial America, Haley-Over, sometimes called Wall Ball, is a kind of Blindman's Buff tag—full of suspense and surprises.

Teams stand on opposite sides of the wall or small building, completely hidden from each other. A player throws the ball over the top to any height and in any direction. If the players on the other side miss the catch, they return the ball over the wall and the volley continues until someone from one of the teams makes a catch.

The player who catches the ball then races around the corner to tag players of the other

team who scatter in all directions. The chaser has 30 seconds to tag a runner by throwing the ball and hitting him, or by chasing and touching him with the ball. The referee calls "Time!" after the 30 seconds is up, and if no one is tagged, the chaser returns to his side.

A tagged runner joins the chasing team on the other side of the wall. Now the chasing team throws the ball over and the routine is repeated.

Haley-Over calls on the honor system, since the throwing team cannot see whether the opposing team caught the ball on the fly. Only then may a player come around to the other side to tag the throwing team.

When all players wind up on one side, the game ends.

Half-Ball Baseball

Players: 6 to 18 in two teams
Materials: Broom-handle bat; hollow rubber ball, cut in half
Surface: Paved

Cutting an old ball in half might seem a little strange, but this provides a fun and challenging twist to an old favorite.

You can make your own half-ball by cutting a Spauldeen ball in half. Find a fine-tooth hacksaw, and get someone to saw it in half for you if you're not familiar with the tool yourself. Some sports stores carry commercial half-balls, if you don't want to fuss with making your own.

Take an old broom handle and wrap one end in masking or electrical tape so that you can get a good grip on it.

After you form two teams and count out to

establish batting order, the batters stand in line while the fielders stand wherever they please, 40 feet (12 m) away. The first batter tosses the half-ball in the air and swings. If he connects, the ball skims through the air like a wobbling Frisbee in anything but a straight line.

Fielders scramble to catch the ball on the fly and put the batter "out." In this game, one bounce on the street counts as a **single** for the batting team; two bounces, a **double**; three bounces, a **triple**; and four bounces a **home run**. If a flying half-ball is strange to see, a bouncing half-ball is stranger. Fielders often collide with one another trying to grab it.

When a batter misses his own toss, he "strikes." After three strikes (an "out") by one or more batters, teams switch sides. The team with the higher score after an agreed-upon amount of time wins the game.

Hen & Chicks

Players: 6 to 12
Materials: None
Surface: Paved or grassy

One player is the Hen, another the Fox. They should be fairly evenly matched. The remaining players are the Chicks. They line up behind the Hen, holding waists or shoulders.

Fox marches up to Hen and says, "Mother Hen, your Chicks look good today." Hen replies, "Mr. Fox, go away!"

Fox then tries to capture the last Chick by pulling her from the line, while Hen tries to protect her. The other Chicks can join in by wrapping themselves around the threatened Chick, but the line must never break apart. If it does, Fox may tag any and all of them.

Each time a Chick is captured, he or she is out of the game—placed in Fox's Cooking Pot. The game ends when all the Chicks are captured—and cooked.

Hit the Coin

Players: 2
Materials: Ball, coin, chalk (optional)
Surface: Paved

This is a great Sunday morning ball game, perfect for those times when you don't want to run around too much and mess up your clothes. Place a coin on the crack between squares in the sidewalk. Or draw two boxes, each 5 feet (1.5 m) square, and separate them with a straight line. One player stands in each box. The object is to bounce the ball on the coin, which scores 1 point. If your ball flips the coin over, you get 2 points and the chance to put the coin back on the dividing line, in case it has been knocked away from you. If you miss the coin completely, you continue to take turns bouncing the ball until someone scores a hit.

The first player to reach a score of 21 wins.

Home Runs

Players: 6 in two teams
Materials: Ball
Surface: Paved; stoop

Home Runs is a short version of baseball, played against a stoop. One player stands in the street just beyond the curb, facing the stoop. He is the "Batter," without a bat. Two teammates stand about 15 feet (4.5 m) behind him, as do all three players from the other team.

The Batter throws the ball against the stoop with as much or as little force as he wishes. A bounce on the sidewalk or out-of-bounds counts as a **strike**. Here's the scoring: 1 bounce in the street—a **single**; 2 bounces—a **double**; 3 bounces—a **triple**; and 4 bounces—a **home run**.

If the ball is caught by someone on the other team, it counts as an automatic **out,** and the teams switch sides.

Keep in mind that no ball may be caught on the fly in the game Home Runs. A ball must bounce at least once before it counts for anything. If your team is "at bat," it can be tough deciding whether to let the ball keep bouncing and risk having the other team nab it, or to snap it up quickly and settle for a lowly single.

Hopscotch

Players: 2 to 6
Materials: Chalk, small stone for each player
Surface: Paved

7	8
6	
4	5
3	
1	2

The game of Hopscotch is very old and has many variations. You can even see the remains of Hopscotch boards scratched into the ancient streets of the Roman Forum! You might know Hopscotch by another name, Potsy. This name probably came about because small pieces of pottery were once tossed onto the board instead of the bottletop or skate key that was used in the 1930s and 1940s.

Hopscotch is an interesting game because it tests your skill and coordination. Some board designs are simple and others are more complex, but they all work the same way. You throw a small object into the first square, hop over that square and through the board to the highest numbered square. Then you turn and hop back through the board. You finish by picking up the object from the first square and hopping *over* it and out.

Let's take an example. If you're playing on an ordinary or standard board, you start out by standing at the foot of the board and tossing your Pot (chip of pottery, skate key, coin, or stone) into the #1 square. If it lands clearly inside, you hop on your right foot into the #2 square, and then into the #3 square. At this point you jump so that you land with your left foot in #4 and your right foot in #5. Then you hop on your right foot into #6, and jump again, landing with your left foot in #7 and your right foot in #8. Now it's time to return. You jump and twist around so that you land facing your Pot— your *left* foot in #8 and your *right* foot in #7. You hop on your *left* foot into #6; jump and land with your left foot in #5 and your right foot in #4; hop

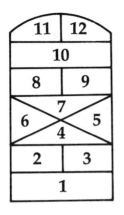

on your left foot into #3; and then into #2. Before you hop out though, you must lean over and pick up your Pot from square #1.

Players take turns throwing the Pot into higher and higher numbered spaces. If a player steps on a line, trips, or if her throw misses its space, the turn passes to the next player. The first player to hop through the full sequence of numbers wins the game.

Some boards are designed with neighboring squares so that you may take turns hopping and jumping (landing on both feet, each one in a separate square).

Territory Hopscotch

Another more elaborate version of Hopscotch uses the Territory rule. After you hop through the board successfully and are standing outside it, you turn your back to it, and toss your coin or stone over your shoulder. Where it lands becomes your Territory, and you write your initials in the corner of the square. The other players may not throw or hop in this square now, which complicates things for everyone! You win if you accumulate more territories than your opponents, or eliminate them by owning enough squares to make hopping too difficult. If you miss the mark or stumble as you try to hop across squares, you are out of the game.

Round Hopscotch

Hopscotch was made for variation. Here are two designs of Round Hopscotch boards.

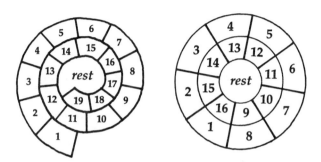

Try designing your own Hopscotch board. It's still Hopscotch as long as you keep to the basic rules of the game.

Horse

Players: 2 to 5
Materials: Basketball
Surface: Basketball court

This enjoyable game developed from one of those improve-your-shot exercises. It's great for warming up, too.

The first player takes a shot from anywhere on the court. If he or she gets the basketball into the basket, the other players must duplicate the same shot from the same location. If they all succeed, the first player makes a second and usually more challenging shot. If one of the other players fails to duplicate the first player's shot, that player gets the letter *H*.

If the first player misses a shot, the second player has the opportunity to make a shot that must be imitated by the other players.

The game continues as players accumulate

letters for missed shots. Players who spell out *HORSE* are out of the game. The remaining player wins.

I Declare War

Players: 5 to 10
Materials: Ball, chalk
Surface: Paved; large, clear area for running

This is a great game for quick thinkers and fast runners. Draw a big circle and divide it up into sections like a pie. Draw a smaller circle in the middle that can (if you're artistic) look like a globe. The slices represent different countries. Each player chooses a "country" and stands in that slice.

Select one player to be IT. If IT is standing in a slice marked Germany, then Germany declares war for this round. IT starts the game holding the ball and saying: "I declare war on ——." Then IT shouts the name of one of the other countries and bounces the ball as hard as possible in the middle circle.

If Germany declares war on France, then everyone (including Germany) runs out of their countries and away from the circle—except France. France stays behind to catch the ball and yell "Freeze!"—stopping the others. France is then allowed to take three giant steps toward the closest player—Italy, perhaps—and throw the ball at him.

If Italy is hit, he becomes IT for the next round. But if France misses, all the players unfreeze and run back to their sections. At this point, France may throw the ball at the running players in a last ditch attempt to find another IT, but if she misses, she returns to her slice and declares war in the next round.

I Declare War Elimination Style

In this version, France forces Italy out of the game if she scores a hit and then may take three more giant steps toward another player and throw the ball again. If she misses hitting the second player, everyone runs back to their countries. The last one home becomes IT in the next round.

Interferers

Players: 6 to 10
Materials: Chalk or rope
Surface: Paved or grassy

In this game the losers get even with the winners. Use rope or chalk to draw starting and finish lines 30 yards (9 m) apart. Players line up behind the starting line, and at the signal, sprint for the finish. The player who comes in last becomes the Interferer who then stands in the way of the others during the next race, running into them and generally disturbing the course of the run. The player who comes in last for this second race now joins the Interferer for the third race, and so on, until only two racers remain and all the others become Interferers.

The single racer who makes it to the other side wins the game.

Johnny on a Pony

Players: 10 or more, an even number
Materials: None
Surface: Grassy; strong tree or wall
   nearby

Divide players evenly into two sides. On one side, players bend over in a line holding waists, with the first player in line bracing himself against a wall or tree trunk. These players make up "the Pony."

One by one, players on the other side jump onto the back of the Pony and wriggle forward to tag the first player in line. Players in the Pony try to shake each rider off before he reaches the first in line, but the Pony must never break apart or collapse.

If the rider makes it far enough to tag the first in line, he gets one point. If thrown off, that player goes to the back of his own team's

line and the Pony gets a point. When 3 points are scored by either side, that team wins and the sides are reversed.

Jump Rope

Players: 1 to 10

Materials: Short jump rope, about 5 feet (1.5 m) long; clothesline at least 20 feet (6 m) long

Surface: Paved

Jumping rope is terrific exercise and a great test of skill and coordination. In old-fashioned May Day celebrations at village fairs, as many as ten people could be seen jumping over one long rope, but you don't often see anything that elaborate these days.

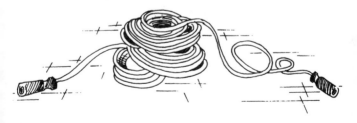

You can jump alone or with a partner, using a short, store-bought jump rope. Or you can jump inside a longer clothesline, turned by two friends. There are two basic classes of games: (1) fancy jumping, chasing, or dancing routines and (2) jump-rope rhymes, which include counting, alphabet, and switching rhymes.

Fancy Jump-Rope Routines

Here are some fancy jump-rope routines. Some involve chasing or dancing.

Rock the Cradle: Rock the rope back and forth instead of making it revolve. You can do this alone on a short rope, or you can do it on a longer rope letting the turners "rock" for you. It's a great way to warm up!

Wind the Clock: While the rope is turning, count from 1 to 12, making a quarter turn clockwise each time. Again, you can do this alone or with two friends turning for you.

Visiting: One player starts jumping alone, turning her own rope. Another player jumps in and faces her, "visiting" for a while, before jumping out again.

Chasing: This involves two turners and at least two jumpers. The first jumper enters, jumps over the rope once, and then rushes out as the second jumper enters, and so on.

Square Dancing: Two players turn while two jumpers approach each other from opposite directions, link arms, and turn once around— all the while jumping!

Hopping: Two players turn as the jumper

rushes in and hops, alternating legs for each turn of the rope. After 10 hops, the jumper runs out and is replaced by another jumper.

Jump-Rope Rhymes

The second class of jump-rope games consists of rhymes—recited by either the turners or the jumpers. There are many kinds of these—some more complicated than others—but most jump-rope rhymes are counting rhymes, alphabet rhymes, or switching rhymes. Here are some samples.

Counting Rhymes

These jump-rope rhymes end with counting, to test how long a jumper can keep going before tripping or making a mistake. The jumper can

chant them alone, or she can have the rope turners chant them for her. One popular counting rhyme goes like this:

> *Fire, fire, house on fire!*
> *Mrs. Sweeny climbed up higher.*
> *There she met the Fireman Steve.*
> *How many kisses did she receive?*
> *One, two, three, four, five, six . . .*

Alphabet Rhymes

The jumper or turners chant the alphabet at the end of these jump-rope rhymes—the letter the jumper stumbles on means something very important. Usually it's said to be the first initial of your sweetheart, whether you know it or not!

> *Strawberry shortcake, cream on top;*
> *Tell me the name of my sweetheart!*
> *A, B, C, D, E . . . .*

Switching

These are short jump-rope rhymes that call for the old jumper to move out and a new one to come in. They are usually chanted by the turners.

> *My mother and your mother*
> *Live across the way.*
> *Every night they have a fight,*
> *And this is what they say:*
> *Acka bake a soda cracker,*
> *Acka bake a few,*
> *Acka bake a soda cracker,*
> *Out goes you!*

Jump-Rope Turning

In addition to the two basic kinds of jump-rope games, there are many ways to *turn* the rope. This can make an already difficult game even more challenging. If you have a very long clothesline, for example, you can turn it into two jump ropes. The clothesline is doubled over. Then one turner holds the two ends, while the other turner wraps the rope around her back, over her forearms, and through her hands. Now you're ready for Double Dutch and French Dutch.

Double Dutch is a technique where the two ropes are turned *toward* each other—but care-

fully—so that they don't collide. The result is a kind of eggbeater, which leaves the poor jumper quite exhausted after a short time!

In **French Dutch,** the ropes are turned away from each other—again, very carefully—with similar results. If this isn't difficult enough, you can try both Double Dutch and French Dutch with a dose of Hot Pepper. **Hop Pepper** means turning the ropes as fast as possible—until someone cries, "Help!"

Kickball

Players: 12 to 18 in two teams
Materials: Medium-size inflated ball; chalk, mats, cardboard, or trash-can lids
Surface: Paved or grassy

Kickball, a kind of no-props baseball, doesn't require highly developed hitting or running skills.

The playing field consists of a baseball diamond with 25 feet (7.5 m) between each of the three bases, adjustable for younger players. You can draw the bases with chalk or use cardboard, mats, or trash-can lids to mark them. One team bats while the other team fields and pitches. The players in the field take the usual positions: one player to each of the three bases, plus at least one infield and one outfield player.

The pitcher rolls the ball to the kicker, who

stands at home plate. The kicker rarely "strikes out" on a rolled ball, so 2 foul balls kicked in succession count as 1 strike. As in baseball, 3 strikes (6 foul balls) make an "out." After three outs, or half an inning, teams switch sides.

When a player kicks the ball, he or she runs for first base while the fielders on the other team scramble to catch the ball and put the runner out in one of these four ways:

- *They can catch a fly ball.*
- *They can throw a ball to the player on first base, who will touch the base before the runner reaches it.*
- *They can tag the runner with the ball.*
- *They can hit the runner by throwing the ball.*

Since an inflated rubber ball will not travel very far when kicked high in the air, and the opposing team can easily catch it, it's best to kick hard and low to the ground. Aim to shoot between fielders.

If a runner makes it home after touching all three bases, he or she scores 1 point for the team.

The team with the most points at the end of nine innings wins the game.

King of the Ring

Players: 4 to 7
Materials: Chalk
Surface: Paved

Draw a circle about 5 feet (1.5 m) in diameter and stand in the center. As the King, you have to protect yourself against invaders, who enter the circle and try to drag you out. Only one invader at a time may enter, and anything goes—pushing, shoving, tripping, lifting up, carrying, or whatever! You'll soon be exhausted enough to want out. That is, after you've tried to hold on to your kingdom for a while. If two invaders enter, you may call "Foul!" and take one of them out of the game. And if three try to gang up on you, you may call "Double foul!" and remove two of them.

Continue playing until everyone has a chance to be King.

Laughing Loop

Players: 5 to 20
Materials: None
Surface: Grassy

The laughter in this game is contagious.

Player #1 lies on his back and places his head on the belly of Player #2. Player #2 then places *his* head on the belly of Player #3, and so on. Players wind up lying in a zigzag formation, but the line should loop around so that the last player places his head on the belly of Player #1.

Now the fun begins. Player #1 shouts, "Ha!" and Player #2 answers with "Ha, ha!" Player #3 shouts, "Ha, ha, ha!" and Player #4 answers with "Ha, ha, ha, ha!" Of course, each time a player says "Ha!" his belly bobs up and down, rocking the next player's head. It's a strange sensation! Soon, everyone loses control and starts laughing hysterically, and round and round it goes!

Limbo

Players: 6 to 10
Materials: Broom or broom handle
Surface: Paved or grassy

Choose two players who will hold opposite ends of the broom. Each end should rest on a player's upturned palm, so that the broom will fall to the ground if bumped from below. Start out with the broom about chest high.

One by one, the other players walk under the broom, making themselves shorter by stretching their legs apart and bending backwards. To get in the spirit, try doing it while the others clap in rhythm. A player who stumbles, or knocks the broom down while going under it, is eliminated.

After all the players go under once, the broom-holders lower the broom to waist level, and the players take turns going under it again. With each repetition, the broom-holders drop the broom a little lower until they have to get on their knees. Eventually, all players but one are eliminated. That one wins the game.

London

Players: 2 to 6

Materials: Chalk; bottle caps or checkers for throwing, one for each player

Surface: Paved

The game London, an unusual combination of Hopscotch and the pencil-and-paper game Hangman, requires patience, patience, patience.

It helps if you're really good friends with the other players.

With chalk, draw a rectangle about 3 feet (1 m) across and 5 feet (1.5 m) deep, and divide it into seven sections. Connect the two corners of the top section with a curved line and write the word *London* in it.

Player #1 stands at the foot of the diagram and throws her bottle cap so that it lands in one of the sections. She draws a small circle (representing a head) in that space, initials it, and throws again. If her bottle cap lands in a different rectangle, she draws another small circle and initials it. If her second or third throw lands in a section she's already initialed, she draws a larger circle (a body) under the smaller one. If the next throw lands in the section with a head and body, she adds a leg, arm, foot, and so on, until she completes a picture of a person. (You need to agree on what constitutes a part with other players before the game begins.) If she lands in the space marked

"London," she can then draw one head in every space or add a body or leg to other "men" already started. Each player throws until his or her piece lands on a line between sections or outside the board.

When a player completes one "man," she begins a new one next to the first. When she completes three "men," she then concentrates on landing her bottle cap in the three-man section again. If she is successful, she draws a line through the three men, adding arms and linking them together. She now "owns" that section. Any player who lands in a section owned by another player loses a turn.

When all the sections are owned, the player with the greatest number of them wins the game.

Losing Your Marbles

Players: 2 to 4

Materials: 10 marbles for each player plus a target marble; stick for marking shoot line, garden spade or old spoon for digging

Surface: Hard packed sand

Dig a small hole about 6 inches (15 cm) in diameter and 2 inches (5 cm) deep. One marble, belonging to neither player, is placed in the hole as a target. Draw a shooting line 15 feet (4.5 m) from the hole. From here, players take turns tossing their marbles with the object of hitting—or banging—the target marble in the hole three times.

The first player to reach that magic number picks up and gets to keep all the marbles that missed. The game continues as players gradually lose their marbles to the winner.

Marbles

How to Shoot a Marble

There are many ways to shoot a marble. Pitching it in the air or bowling it across the ground, two of the easier techniques, require little practice. But a true marble player's method of shooting—a must if you're playing a game like Ringer—is called "knuckling down."

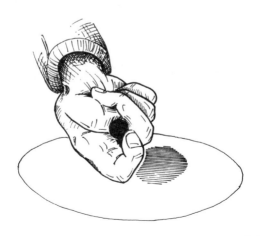

To knuckle down, turn your hand palm up and place all of your knuckles (except your thumb) on the ground. Place the marble between the tip and the first joint of your first finger and hold it there by pressing against it with the nail of your thumb. When you're ready to shoot, flick your thumb outward, propelling the marble. Watch it fly!

Try out various games of Marbles with your friends—Losing Your Marbles, Poison, and Ringer.

Monday, Tuesday

Players: 7
Materials: Ball
Surface: Paved; high wall

Here's a game to test your reflexes. Play it when you're razor-sharp and full of energy!

Each player takes the name of a day in the week. The first player (Friday) throws the ball against the ground as hard as possible so that it bounces up and rebounds against the wall. At the same time, Friday shouts out the day-name of another player—Wednesday, let's say—who must catch the ball after the first bounce and send it back in the same way, calling out the name of another player.

If Wednesday misses the catch, everyone scatters except Wednesday, who must now retrieve the ball and tag one of the others. The tagged player is next to throw the ball against the ground, but the tag counts as a mark against him. Three tags and a player is out of the game altogether. The game continues until only one player is left—the winner.

Nine Men's Morris

Players: 2

Materials: Chalk; 9 coins or stones for
   each player (players must be able to tell
   their pieces apart)

Surface: Paved

How old is this game? It was a favorite in the
16th century among country folk during
Shakespeare's time. The Bard even mentions it
by name in his play *A Midsummer Night's
Dream.* Supposedly, William Shakespeare himself was an accomplished player!

Nine Men's Morris may remind you a little
of Tic-Tac-Toe or checkers, but it has a charm
all its own. Draw a board consisting of three
concentric squares. Each square should contain
eight dots—for a total of 24 dots.

The players each have nine coins or stones
that they take turns placing one by one, over

the dots. Make sure that whatever pieces you use for playing are easy to distinguish from your opponent's pieces.

When you finish placing all the pieces on the board, take turns moving your pieces to neighboring empty points. The object is to form a row of three—either diagonally or along the side of a square—without being blocked by an opponent.

When you form a row of three, you may remove one of your opponent's pieces from the board. This holds true only for your opponent's unconnected pieces. Once a player forms a row of three, no pieces of it may be removed.

However, there is one exception to this rule: a piece may be removed from a row *only* if no other pieces are available. When this happens, the game is over, and the player who has lost the piece loses the game. Another way to win is to block all of your opponent's men, making it impossible for him to move.

Nine Pins

Players: 2 to 5

Materials: 9 plastic soda-pop bottles, all roughly equal in size and filled with enough sand to make them stable; croquet ball

Surface: Paved

Nine Pins is an old-fashioned bowling game. You need a slightly heavy, nonbouncing ball, like a wooden croquet ball. Place nine bottles like this:

The object of the game is to bowl over the bottles in the circle without knocking over the

center bottle, which is called the Jack. Each bottle counts 2 points, except for the Jack, which has no point value.

Take turns. You may walk around the circle, but you are never allowed to get closer than 12 feet (3.6 m). If you knock down one or more bottles on a single bowl, they are turned upright again, and you get another turn. But if you knock over the Jack, you must add up the point values of all the bottles you just knocked over and deduct them from your total score. Knocking down the Jack also ends your turn. A score of 21 wins.

If a player knocks over all eight bottles during a single turn without knocking over the Jack, he gets a 10-point bonus, and his turn is over.

Sample Game

Here's a sample game of Nine Pins with two players, Steve and Jill. Steve knocks down two bottles, but misses the Jack on his first turn. He gets 4 points and may bowl again. He knocks over a bottle *and* the Jack on his second turn, so he deducts 2 points from his total score of 4 points, which leaves him with 2 points and ends his turn. Now Jill tries. She knocks over a bottle and the Jack in her first turn and is given a **negative score**, –2 (minus two) points. It's Steve's turn again. This time Steve's bowl is a disaster—three bottles tumble over, taking the Jack with them.

The three bottles add up to a score of –6 for that turn. Steve had a score of 2, so he winds up with a score of –4 points, giving Jill an odd sort of lead. For the next turns, Steve and Jill bowl cautiously, inching their way toward a winning 21.

Down the Lane

For a more challenging game, place the bottles no more than 10 inches (25 cm) away from the

Jack. Bowl "down the lane" at the bottles—that is, from behind a line about 15 feet (4.5 m) away. The same bonus-point rule applies for knocking over all the bottles during a single turn.

Pass-the-Grapefruit Relay

Players: 10 to 20 in two teams

Materials: 2 large grapefruits, cold
  if possible

Surface: Paved or grassy

You're probably familiar with Pass the Grapefruit, a popular party game in which a grapefruit is passed under the chin from player to
player. In this relay race, the grapefruit is carried by each racer, who then passes it to his
waiting teammate—all under the chin. But with
this version, there's another twist at the end . . .

Mark out starting and finish lines and
place them 10 yards (9 m) apart. Divide each
team in half so that five racers line up behind
the starting line and the other five line up
behind the finish line. A grapefruit is placed
behind the starting line at the foot of each
team's first racer.

At the "Go!" signal, the first racer jumps down on all fours and picks up the grapefruit by tucking it under his chin—no hands! He stands up with the grapefruit, clasps his hands behind his back, and runs across to the finish line where his teammate waits. If he drops his grapefruit, he must drop down on all fours to pick it up again. Behind the finish line, teammates pass the grapefruits under the chin. The first racer goes to the end of the line, and the second racer runs back to the starting line to pass his grapefruit to the third racer, and so on. When the last racer passes his grapefruit back to the first, or original, racer, both halves of the team run from opposite sides of the field and combine to make one line, ten players long (or as many players as are on the team).

Now it's pass-the-grapefruit time. The first racer passes his grapefruit to the next in line, who passes it to the next in line. The last person in line to receive the grapefruit shouts "Time!" winning the game for his team.

Pigs to Market

Players: 2 to 10

Materials: Chalk or rope; broom handles or
long sticks for each player; plastic soda-pop
bottles with caps for each player; sand to fill
each bottle

Surface: Paved or grassy

This racing game is tougher than it sounds,
especially when you have more than three
players—all of them zigzagging in a mad dash
for the finish line.

Fill each soda-pop bottle with sand and
screw the cap on. Each bottle is a Pig. Mark
starting and finish lines with chalk or rope.
Players stand beside each other holding broom
handles. Place a Pig in front of each player, on
its side. At the starting signal, the players
must push their Pigs along quickly with the

broomsticks, trying to race in a straight line and keep out of each other's way. That's easier said than done!

The first player to reach the finish line wins the game.

Poison

Players: 2 to 5

Materials: 20 marbles per player;
   stick; garden spade or old spoon

Surface: Hard-packed sand

Poison gives a good marbles player the chance
to become truly deadly.

Use a garden spade or old spoon to dig a
shallow hole with a diameter of about 5 inches
(12.5 cm). This is the Poison Pot, and each
player drops a marble into it. Next, use a stick
to draw a circle around the hole with a radius
of about 3 feet (1 m) from the hole's edge. This
is called the Poison Ring. The setup is complete
when players place additional marbles within
the ring—2 each—in a circular formation
around the Poison Pot.

Players knuckle down 5 feet (1.5 m) from
the ring and shoot to see who comes closest to

the ring's edge without going over the line. The most accurate shot entitles the shooter to take a place just outside the ring and begin the game.

Part One

The rules of Poison dictate that a player must shoot a marble out of the ring, and his shooter marble must also leave the ring. Marbles that leave the ring become his property and count as 1 point each. If he fails—by missing a target, or if his shooting marble remains inside— he surrenders to the Poison Pot all of the marbles he won on that turn, and the turn is over. If he fails on the first attempt and has no winning marbles to surrender, he must pay a penalty of two marbles to the Poison Pot.

When a sharp-shooting player collects ten marbles and scores 10 points, he calls out "Poison!" and the game pauses. He distributes his ten marbles among the other players, who

remove the rest of their marbles from the ring
and wait for the next part of the game.

Part Two

The Poison Player now removes all the marbles in the Poison Pot and places them around
the outside of the ring. Then each remaining
player, one by one, is called to place all his
marbles inside the ring as targets for the
Poison Player.

The Poison Player shoots, without inter-
ruption, his poison marbles from outside the
ring, bumping and eliminating the other player's marbles. If the Poison Player misses, the
player who is his target gets to remove his
remaining marbles from the ring and the *next*
player is called to throw in *his* marbles.

It might seem like an excruciating way to
wind down a game—the remaining players
would have little hope of saving their marbles

from the Poison Player—if it weren't for one trick rule. If the Poison Player accidentally shoots a marble into the Poison Pot, he is no longer "poison," and his victim becomes the new Poison Player—taking whatever marbles remain in the center and arranging them, just as the first Poison Player did—outside the ring. Now this *new* Poison Player calls for the remaining players to toss all their marbles into the ring.

The game continues until one Poison Player—the winner—collects all the marbles.

Pyramid Building

Players: 10 to 15
Materials: None
Surface: Grassy

Pyramid building is harder than it sounds. You need some strong backs and some good balancers. The reward is a magnificent human structure—short-lived though it may be!

The biggest players should make up the bottom row. If you're playing with ten people, the bottom row should be four players across—each on hands and knees and very close to his neighbor. The next row is made up of three players, also on hands and knees and packed close together. Each player in the second row straddles the crack between players in the bottom row, placing each knee on a separate player. The third row has two players, who straddle in the same way, and at the top of the pyramid is a single player.

Try taking your pyramid apart carefully, and then putting it back together with a different combination of players. But if you can't resist, and no one objects—let it crumble!

Red Light, Green Light

Players: 5 to 10
Materials: Chalk or rope
Surface: Paved or grassy

One player, IT, moves about 15 feet (4.5 m) away from the others, who stand in a row at the starting line, which you can mark with chalk or a rope.

IT turns his back to the others and calls "Green Light!" which signals to the players that they can run toward him. After a few seconds, he calls "Red Light!" which tells running players they must stop and freeze in position. IT then whirls around to face the players and tries to catch someone moving. If caught, that player must return to the starting line.

Each time IT turns his back and calls "Green Light!" the players run closer. As they close in, IT usually makes green lights shorter and red lights longer, hoping to catch the closest player and send him back to the starting line.

The player who manages to tag IT becomes IT in the next game.

Red Rover

Players: 7 to 20

Materials: Chalk or 2 ropes for marking boundary lines

Surface: Paved or grassy; large area

Red Rover is a classic outdoor game. Some versions are nearly 700 years old.

Divide a 100-foot (30-m) stretch of the closed street or yard into three equal areas. The outer areas are Dens, while the middle area is occupied by a single player. The other players may go into either Den; each player can choose which Den to start from.

All the players wait in their Dens until the middle player begins the game by calling: "Red Rover, Red Rover, come on over!" Then all run from their Dens across the middle area to seek safety in the opposite Den. The middle player tries to capture one of the players by holding him and counting to 10. If he succeeds, the captured player remains in the middle and helps capture the remaining players in the next round.

The middle players call, "Red Rover, Red Rover, come on over!" a second time, and the remaining players run across again. As you can see, each time the call is repeated, more players are captured, and fewer players are left to occupy the Dens. This may result in one Den being left empty. If this happens, one of the middle players may rush into the empty Den and shout, "Take base 1–2–3!" three times.

From that point on, the game is slightly different. Middle players, still in position, are now allowed to choose individual players ("Red Rover, Red Rover, call Jackie over!") to run across their territory. If one very fast runner is particularly irksome to the middle players, you can bet that they'll pick him first to run across. That player may ask for "protection"—that is, he may ask up to three other runners to surround him as he makes a dash for it, but no player has to help him.

When the last runner is captured by the middle players, the game is over. Usually this last runner, by virtue of his skill and longevity, gets to choose someone to call, "Red Rover, Red Rover, come on over!" and begin the next game.

Ringelevio 1-2-3

Players: 10 to 30, an even number

Materials: Chalk or rope

Surface: Paved or grassy; large area, with a few small obstacles, like trees, bushes, hydrants

You need lots of room for this rough-and-tumble tag game. The teams need to do some fast running.

Select two teams and mark out a Den that is large enough to hold an entire team. One team goes out while the other—the IT team—stays near, but not inside, the Den. The IT team chooses one of its members to guard the Den, which is done by keeping one foot inside the Den at all times.

The game begins when the IT team starts counting to 100, giving the field team enough time to run far away from the Den. When the count is finished, the IT team shouts, "Ready or not, here we come!" and everyone on the team, except for the Den Guard, runs after the others.

To capture a player, a member of the IT team must grab and hold onto his victim long enough to call out, "Ringelevio 1–2–3!" three times. If the victim breaks away before this chant is completed, he may continue running. If he's captured, however, he's placed in the Den and made prisoner.

Captured players remain in the Den until tagged by a teammate. They may also break out if the Den Guard accidentally takes one foot out of the Den or places *both* feet inside it. Prisoners may try to pull the Guard inside, or push him out, or they may just wait to be rescued.

If an IT player gets tired, he can stand alongside the Den next to the Guard. But if that tired player steps into the Den accidentally, or if he is pulled into it by one of the prison-

ers, the prisoner may shout out "Two Guards!" and win his own release.

When all the members of the field team are captured, the game is over. Change sides for the next game.

Ringer

Players: 2 to 6

Materials: 13 ordinary marbles; 2 to 6
  shooter marbles, depending on the number
  of players; chalk or stick

Surface: Paved or hard dirt

This is the most widely played marble game, and it provides a good opportunity to bone up on shooting techniques.

Using chalk or a stick, draw a ring on the ground, 10 feet (3 m) in diameter. With the center of the ring as a point of intersection, draw two lines, each 2 feet (0.6 m) long, at right angles to form a cross. Place a marble at the center and three marbles on each of the four lines of the cross, each marble no less than 3 inches (7.5 cm) from the next one.

To win, a player must knock seven marbles out of the ring while keeping his shooting marble inside the ring. He takes the first shot from any point outside the ring and continues shooting until he either wins, misses, or shoots out of the ring. If he doesn't win on the first try—and he usually doesn't—replace the marbles and let the next player take a turn.

For each new turn, a player takes his first shot from any point outside the ring. And of course, all shots are performed "knuckles down" to count.

Rooster Fight

Players: 6 to 20, an even number, in pairs

Materials: Handkerchiefs or scarves, one for every other player

Surface: Paved or grassy

Rooster Fight is a perfect name for this Mexican favorite. Every player tucks a handkerchief behind a belt or in a pocket—in a place where it can't be snatched away easily. Players pair off, facing their partners. Then each player holds his right arm up against his chest (grasping his left shoulder with his right hand), hops on the right foot, and tries to steal his partner's handkerchief. Partners must always face each other and may never run away. Pushing and bumping is allowed, but if a player drops his arm, or if his foot touches the ground, he is disqualified and out of the game.

When your handkerchief is stolen, you are out of the game. Winners wait for everyone to finish, and then they pair off for a final challenge.

Run, Sheepy, Run!

Players: 10 to 20, an even number

Materials: Chalk or rope

Surface: Paved or grassy; a large playing
area with many good places to hide

Try this game if you like signals and secret codes. Divide the players into two teams and mark out two home bases. Also mark out a Prison, which should be far away from each home base. In this game, one team hides and then tries to return to home base before the other team can find and capture its members. Both teams choose captains who direct the hiding and searching.

Before you start, the Captain of the Hiders decides on a secret code that will allow him to communicate important information to his teammates. Some code words might be:

Bloodhound, which means "They're closing in on you; keep low and stay quiet."

Grandma, which means "It's safe to start crawling toward home now."

House on Fire, which means "Run for it!"

The Captain can make up as many code words as he'd like, but it's best to keep them simple to avoid confusion.

After the team of Hiders learns the code, their Captain announces that his team is ready to hide. The team of Searchers wait at home base and don't look. Meanwhile, the Captain of the Hiders goes with hiding team members and notes their hiding places. Team members should hide fairly close by so that they can hear the code words. When everyone is hidden, the Captain of the Hiders returns to the Search team and announces that all is ready.

The search begins. Both team captains take part: the Captain of the Searchers leads the search, and the Captain of the Hiders calls out code words to teammates, trying to maneuver them closer to home. He tells them when it's safe to creep forward or when it's better to stay back. The Captain of the Searchers may try to confuse the hiding players by calling out the same code words!

If one of the Hiders is discovered by one of the Searchers, the Hider is captured and placed in Prison.

Captured players are released only when tagged by a teammate.

When the Captain of the Hiders feels he has guided his team close enough to home, he calls out, "Run, Sheepy, Run!" which means that everyone can come out of hiding and make a run for it. This also means that the search is over, and the Searchers must also run for home. Captured players in Prison must be tagged and released by their teammates at this time. The first team to get all of its players safely within home base wins the game.

The Captain of the Searchers may also call out, "Run, Sheepy, Run!" too. He may do this if he feels his team is in a better position to win the race for home, which might be the case if some of the fastest runners on the hiding team have been captured.

Teams take turns being the Hiders and the Searchers. And of course, for each game a new secret code must be invented.

Sardines

Players: 5 to 10
Materials: Chalk or rope
Surface: Paved or grassy; a moderately
    large area with lots of nooks and crannies

This is hide-and-seek backwards, with a good chase at the end. Mark out home base, or choose any clearly marked spot for it. Select one player to be IT, but in this game IT hides while *the others* count to 50. When the count is through, the players go out in search of IT, quickly separating from each other to look thoroughly in every part of the area. When one of the searchers spots IT, however, he doesn't tag her or call out to the others, but instead joins her in her space, squeezing in like a sardine next to her. As the remaining searchers discover the hiders, each squeezes into the hiding place. Everyone must now be especially quiet so as not to alert the remaining searchers. That's easier said than done!

The hiding players wait for the last searching player, who is usually getting pretty nervous by this time. When he finally discovers the hiding sardines, they all jump out and race for home base. The last player to reach home base becomes IT in the next game.

Seven-Up

Players: 1
Materials: Rubber ball, chalk
Surface: Paved; high wall

This handball game has seven steps, with each step a little more complicated than the one before. You play it alone, with the Wall as your only real opponent. Draw a line about 5 feet (1.5 m) from the base of a wall, and stand behind it. Then start with the first step, "onesies."

For **onesies,** throw the ball against the wall and catch it on the fly.

For **twosies,** throw the ball against the wall, but let it bounce once in front of the line before you catch it. Repeat.

For **threesies,** throw the ball against the wall and clap before you catch it on the fly. Repeat this two more times.

For **foursies,** throw the ball against the wall, spin around, and catch it after the first bounce. Repeat this three more times, alternating the direction of your spin.

For **fivesies,** throw the ball against the wall, clap twice behind your back, and catch it on the fly. Repeat this four more times.

For **sixies,** throw the ball against the wall, get down in a push-up position, then jump up and catch the ball after the first bounce. Repeat only two more times. (Thank goodness!)

For **sevensies,** throw the ball against the wall, clap your hands once in front and once in back, before catching the ball on the fly. Repeat this six more times.

Scoring

Each step and repetition that you complete counts as 1 point. If you go all the way from onsies to sevensies without a mistake, you've

collected 25 points and win the game. But each
miss gives the Wall a point, too. Usually, by the
time you've reached sevensies, the score is
something like: You—18 points; Wall—7 points.
In this case, you continue the game, from onesies on until either you or the Wall reaches a
score of 25. Make sure that the Wall plays fair.

Shadow Tag

Players: 4 to 10
Materials: None
Surface: Paved or grassy

The twist in this tag game is that IT has to step on the shadow of a runner to tag him. Of course, playing at different times of day will have different results—high noon and small shadows make for a harder game, and late afternoon shadows give IT a decided advantage.

The interesting thing about Shadow Tag is that you get involved in a whole new way of running. If IT stands in front of you, but your shadow lies behind, you can practically march up to IT and tweak his nose! Watching out for your shadow instead of for yourself also makes for collisions between players—so be careful.

Shadow Freeze Tag

In this variation, IT tags your back to freeze you, but any other player can tag your shadow to *unfreeze* you. At first, it might seem easier tagging shadows than backs, but that all depends on the time of day.

Skin the Snake

Players: 5 to 20
Materials: None
Surface: Grassy

You don't have to be a contortionist to play Skin the Snake. In fact, with a little practice, it's really a cinch. Players stand in line, one

behind the other, and bend forward. Each player puts his right hand between his legs and grabs the left hand of the player in back of him. When everyone has a firm grip, the players walk slowly backwards. The player at the rear of the line lies on his back while one by one, the rest of the players straddle him and lie down behind him.

After you finish skinning the snake, you might want to put it back together again. The last player to lie down gets up and walks astride the line, pulling up the next player—until everyone is back in line again.

Skully

Players: 2 to 7

Materials: Chalk; bottle caps or checkers;
   chewing gum (optional)

Surface: Paved and smooth

Skully is a little like Marbles, except that you play with bottle caps or checkers. If you're smart, you'll have some sticky chewing gum around for this one. (It'll come in handy later.) Draw a board no more than 5 feet (1.5 cm) from end to end. Make sure the pavement you draw on isn't too bumpy to skate a bottle cap across.

The object of Skully is to flick (snap your index finger out from under your thumb) a bottle cap from Box #1 all the way to Box #13, and then back to Box #1 again. When you return to Box #1, you become a Killer and can take a player out of the game by bumping his bottle cap with yours.

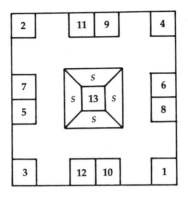

You begin the game by taking turns flicking a bottle cap through the board from square to square. You are not allowed to take shortcuts through the other squares. Surrounding Box #13 are four Skull Zones. If you land in any one of them, you must go through the other three before you can enter Box #13.

If you can possibly bump another player's bottle cap, it is highly recommended. That not only knocks him out of position, but it gives you an extra turn. However, you may "gum your cap" (or checker) to keep it sticking to the pavement when you see trouble coming, and then remove the gum when it's your turn to shoot. It's perfectly legal in this game!

Often, the last stages of the Skully involve several Killer bottle caps. You're the winner when you eliminate everyone else.

Sleeping-Bag Relay Race

Players: 16 to 30 in two teams

Materials: 2 sleeping bags; rope or wooden stakes to mark starting and finish lines

Surface: Grassy or sandy

This is a variation on one of the simplest and most popular of picnic relay races—the burlap-bag or potato-sack race. Sleeping bags are even more fun because they're bulky and harder to "steer." Most are also deep enough to swallow

an unwary racer after the first few hops—to the delight of the competition.

With wooden stakes or rope, mark starting and finish lines 15 yards (13.5 m) apart. You can adjust this distance for smaller players if necessary. All players remove their shoes, and each team divides in half, so that there are two lines of at least four players facing each other from opposite ends of the racing field.

The first players of each team wait behind the starting line with a sleeping bag beside them on the ground. At the "Go!" signal, they pick up the bags, climb in, and hop across the field to waiting teammates. Bags are handed over only after the original racers cross the finish line. The second racers hop back across to the starting line and turn the bags over to the third racers; the third racers hop back to the finish line and give their bags to the fourth racers, and so on.

The first team to have the last racer hop back across the starting line wins the race.

Smugglers

Players: 10 to 20, an even number

Materials: A key, stone, coin, or any other small object; chalk or rope for marking out a Den

Surface: Paved or grassy; a large, not necessarily flat, area to make the chase more interesting

You need two teams for this game: the Ins and the Outs. The Ins have a Den while the Outs plan their strategy in the field.

One member of the Outs has the "jewel," which can be a key, a stone, a coin—anything small enough to be hidden in the palm of your hand. The identity of the player who carries the jewel must remain a closely guarded secret among teammates.

The Ins count to 50 while the Outs move

farther and farther away. After the count is finished, the Ins yell, "Smugglers!" and the chase is on. As each member of the Out team is tagged, he must open his hands to show whether or not he has the jewel. Of course, the jewel should be passed around among teammates as quickly and as inconspicuously as possible. There are lots of opportunities for playing the decoy in this game!

When the holder of the jewel is tagged, the game is over and the sides change.

Smuggler Elimination Game

You may want to try playing Smugglers with the rule that a tagged player who does *not* have the jewel is taken out of the game. This makes for fewer and fewer players on the Out team, and it becomes more difficult to smuggle the jewel undetected. But if tagged players are allowed to stay in the game and keep running, you'll get some interesting results, because the jewel can continue to be passed almost anywhere. Your choice!

The Snake Eats Its Tail

Players: 10 to 30
Materials: None
Surface: Paved or grassy

In this game the Snake has some unexpected twists and turns. Everyone joins hands, making a long line. Or, if you prefer, you can hold waists or shoulders instead—it doesn't really matter. The idea of this game is that the head of this Snake (the first person in line) tries to

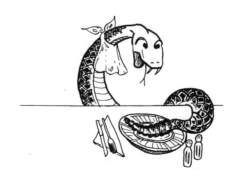

tag the last player in line, eliminating him. The players in between squirm around, trying to keep head and tail apart. Any player who breaks the line is out.

The game continues until the Snake swallows the last morsel of tail, or until everyone is too dizzy to continue playing.

Snap the Whip

Players: 7 to 20
Materials: None
Surface: Paved or grassy; a large area

This game is everyone's favorite. The longer the line of players, the wilder the ride—especially for the player at the end!

Everyone lines up, holding hands. The first player in line runs as fast as he can, dragging the others behind him. He tries to "snap the whip" by making lots of sharp turns. Any player who breaks the line is eliminated. Play until everyone is tired!

Spud

Players: 4 to 10
Materials: Medium-size inflated ball
Surface: Paved

Players may either take numbers or use their own names. All form a circle around one player who has the ball. That player throws the ball straight up into the air and calls the number or name of another player. Everyone scatters except for the named player, who catches the ball and calls out "Spud!"—freezing all the others.

The named player now takes three giant steps to the closest frozen player and attempts to "tag" him by throwing or rolling the ball. If successful, the tagged player gets the letter *S* and throws the ball in the next round.

If the thrower misses her target, she gets an *S* and tries again. The second, third, and fourth time players either get tagged or miss tagging someone with the ball, they get the letters *P, U,* and *D,* respectively. Any player to spell *SPUD* is out of the game.

Continue playing until all but two players remain. The first to eliminate the other player wins the game.

Steal the Bacon

Players: 11 to 31; 5 to 15 on a team,
   plus a referee
Materials: An object to represent the
   "bacon"—hat, shoe, ball, etc.; chalk or rope
   for marking boundary lines
Surface: Paved or grassy

This old-time favorite is fun to play anywhere—even in a gym when rain prevents taking recess outside. Both older and younger
children can play at the same time.

   Draw a rectangular playing area 20 × 40 feet
(6 × 12 m) and place the "bacon" in the center.
Divide the players into two teams. Line up each
team behind the narrow edges of the rectangle at
opposite sides, 40 feet (12 m) apart. Players
stand about 3 feet (1 m) apart and each team
counts off so that every player has a number.

The game begins when the referee, who stands in the middle—but to the side of the playing area—calls out a number. The players from both teams who have the same number dash out to "steal the bacon." The player who carries the bacon back to his team without being tagged by the other player gains 1 point. If the player with the bacon is tagged, the tagger's team receives 1 point.

The first team to accumulate 25 points wins the game.

Stoop Ball

Players: 1 or 2
Materials: Ball, chalk
Surface: Paved; a porch stoop

Stoop Ball is a great game for a lazy afternoon. You can play it alone or with a partner.
If you're playing by yourself, stand in the
street a few feet (about 1 m) from the curb,
and throw the ball at the Stoop. There are two
ways to score:

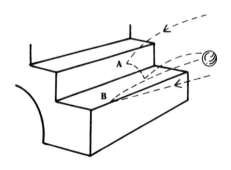

Riser Ball: The ball hits the back of the step (the *riser*), ricochets back down against the step, and you catch it on the fly. (See movement A in diagram.) This earns you 1 point.

Corner Ball: The ball hits the corner where the step and the riser join, bounces back, and you catch it on the fly. (See movement B in diagram.) This earns you 10 points.

If your ball bounces back to you in any way other than a Riser Ball or Corner Ball, or if you fail to catch the ball on the fly, the Stoop scores 1 point. It's a contest between you and the Stoop. The first one to reach a score of 100 points wins.

Stoop Ball for Two Players

When you play Stoop Ball with two players, give point values to each step. The bottom step can count 5 points, the step above it 10 points, the step above that 15 points, and so on for as many steps as there are.

You throw the ball the same way, except that this time it must bounce once before it is caught. A successful corner ball gives you a whopping 25-point bonus! But beware. If your opponent catches your ball, he can steal these points from you, and any ball is fair game for both. A foul or missed ball means no points for anyone. The first player to reach 100 points wins.

Tee Ball

Players: 18 in two teams
Materials: Softball; bat; 3-foot- (0.9-m-) long cardboard tube or a commercial Tee; trash-can covers or cardboard for marking bases
Surface: Sandy or grassy

Tee Ball is a great introduction to baseball because it teaches young players the rules of the game and helps them develop skills necessary for playing it. No team wins or loses, which allows beginning players to enjoy learning the basics—batting, throwing, catching, and fielding—without the pressures of competing.

Little League stores sell the rubber Tee, but for an inexpensive substitute, you can remove the cardboard tube from a roll of gift wrap and place the end in a soft mound of sand where the batter swings. The tee should stand about 3 feet (1 m) high, tip over easily when the batter hits the ball from the top, and substitute for pitched throws.

Scale the playing field to fit younger players: 60 feet (18 m) between bases and 46 feet (13.8 m) between home plate and the pitcher's mound. Teams take turns batting or fielding. The fielders having the usual nine positions as follows:

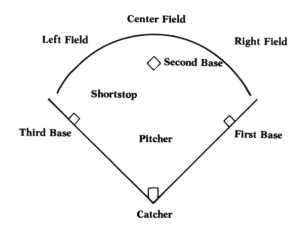

Each player may keep his field position for the entire game, or players can trade positions for variety.

As in baseball, teams score points when the batter hits the ball and runs through the bases. A player may run only when he or a teammate hits the ball. Runners who make it through all three bases and back to home plate score a point for their team. Unlike baseball, however, points measure a team's progress in learning basic batting skills, except nothing is tallied— no team wins or loses.

The fielding team attempts to tag out a batter by either catching the ball "on the fly" (before it hits the ground) or by catching it after it rolls or bounces and throwing it to a teammate on the base the runner is approaching. For instance, if the third baseman catches the ball and tags the runner before he reaches third base, the runner is out and the batting team scores no point. If the runner touches third base before the baseman can catch the ball and tag him, he continues to home plate and scores a point for his team. In this way, fielders may tag runners "out" on any base, including home plate, by throwing the ball to the catcher.

In regulation baseball, three "strikes" (three pitched balls missed by the batter) count as an "out." In Tee Ball, however, every player up to bat swings as many times as he or she likes until connecting with the ball. The next in line then takes a turn. When everyone on the batting team makes a successful hit, the teams switch sides.

When a team bats once and plays the field once, this makes up an inning. Play four innings—six at most. The usual nine innings tend to exhaust younger players.

Three-Legged Relay

Players: 16 to 40 in two teams, an even number

Materials: 2-foot (60-cm) lengths of rope or cloth for each racing pair; rope or wooden stakes for marking starting and finish lines

Surface: Grassy

Here's a relay race guaranteed to keep both players and watchers in stitches. You may want to practice the three-legged walk with your partner before you try it in the tournament, but part of the fun in Three-Legged Relay is never getting it quite right!

With wooden stakes or rope, mark 15-foot (4.5-m) starting and finish lines at opposite ends of the racing field, about 20 yards (18 m) apart. The players of each team line up in pairs, one pair behind the other, and the two teams stand 7 feet (2 m) apart.

Now for the fun. Each pair of players must "share a leg"—that is, the inside ankle of each player is tied to his partner's inside ankle. Use the short length of rope or cloth for this, making sure that you tie it tight enough to stay on during the race, but not so tight that it's uncomfortable.

At the "Go!" signal, pairs of players from competing teams race forward toward the finish line—each player struggling to control this "shared leg" with his racing partner. It takes a while before you get the hang of it, and a few initial moments of spinning, tripping, or just plain flopping to the ground in exasperation are to be expected.

After the players cross the finish line, they turn and race back to tag the second pair of players on their team. The second pair hobbles across and back to tag the third pair, and so on. The winner is the first team to tag its original pair of players.

Whip Ball

Players: 3 to 11 in two teams; referee
Materials: 3-foot (l-m) length of old garden
hose; pink rubber handball; chalk for draw-
ing home plate
Surface: Paved

This abbreviated version of baseball has the
added oddity of a flexible bat. Don't laugh until
you've tried it!

One player, the batter, stands sideways on
home plate with arms down, holding the hose
with one hand and the ball with the other.
When he is ready to bat, he extends his throwing arm and tosses the ball straight up at a distance of about 3 feet (1 m) from his body. He
swings the hose wide with his batting arm,
connecting with the ball as it descends. Then,
whap! Unlike a rigid bat, a flexible bat bends
backwards during the initial stage of the

swing, but whips forward for the later, or connecting, stage. The result can be a ball that sails far and wide!

The players from the other team stand 15 yards (13.5 m) from the batter and try to catch the ball before it bounces. One bounce counts as a single for the batter's team; two bounces, a double; three bounces, a triple; and four bounces, a home run. If the ball is caught on the fly by the fielding team, it counts as an automatic out and the teams switch sides. The referee tallies runs and keeps an accurate score.

The first team to score 21 points wins the game.

Whirligig

Players: 5 to 10

Materials: Long rope, at least 6 feet (1.8 m) long; old shoe

Surface: Paved or grassy

In this game, a Whirligig is a long piece of rope with an old shoe tied to one end for weight. One player holds the other end of the rope and spins around, so that the rope makes a sweep-

ing circular motion. You'll see that even though the center player is standing, the weighted end of the rope swings close to the ground. The other players jump over the rope as it sweeps past them, and they are eliminated if they stumble. The center player may spin faster, bringing the rope higher. Everyone has to keep up!

Take turns spinning the rope.

Indoor &
Outdoor Games

Blindman's Buff

Players: 4 to 10
Materials: Blindfold
Surface: Paved or grassy

This is one of the oldest games in Western culture, and it really hasn't changed much over the centuries. Just imagine this: you'll be playing the ten-zillionth game of Blindman's Buff in almost exactly the same way people played it more than a thousand years ago.

Blindfold one player and spin him around three times. The blindfolded player tries to tag another player, who may tease and taunt him. For instance, the other players may crouch low, sneak up behind the Blindman, and yell "Boo!" or they may stand still and keep very quiet.

Eventually, though, someone will get careless and be tagged. That player is then blindfolded for the next game.

Brother Bob

Players: 6 or more; Leader
Materials: 2 blindfolds, 2 chairs, pillow

This game comes from the heyday of college fraternity pranks. The original version used a paddle! We'll substitute a soft pillow.

The Leader seats two blindfolded players back to back. The remaining players surround the blindfolded players. But before blindfolding the two, the Leader shows them the pillow that one of the other players would smack them with. So each blindfolded player is challenged to guess his smacker.

But this is a prank, and one of the blindfolded players knows it. He'll help the others fool the unknowing player. After the blindfolded players sit, Player #1 quietly takes off his blindfold, grabs the pillow, and smacks himself in the head. Then he says, "Brother Bob, I've been bobbed!" "Who bobbed you?" asks Player #2. The first player pretends to guess a name and discover his smacker. Then he takes the pillow and smacks his blindfolded partner. While Player #2 says "Brother Bob, I've been bobbed!" Player #1 slips the blindfold back on (the Leader can help) and takes his seat. "Who bobbed you?" he asks Player #2.

Now Player #2 starts guessing, but each player he names denies smacking him. At this point, he'll probably rip off his blindfold to look at the company. Of course, Player #1, still blindfolded, will look as guiltless as ever. But by the process of elimination, Player #1 will soon discover who really "bobbed" him.

Bubble Relay Race

Players: 2 to 20 in teams
Materials: Bubble soap and bowl for each
   player or team, straw for each player, nonslip rubber-sole shoes
Surface: Smooth floor or outdoor patio

You can vary the number of players in this game. As a simple race, it requires only two players. As a relay race, it can include a large number of players in several teams, depending on the indoor or outdoor space available.

Mark starting lines at opposite sides of the space. You can do this by placing two books on the floor and imagining a line drawn between them. To avoid slipping, make sure each player wears rubber-sole shoes or any type of shoe that grips the floor. Bubble Relay must be played on a smooth indoor surface or outdoor patio to avoid spilling soap on a carpeted floor.

For the team relay version, divide each team in half and line the players up at opposite sides of the room. Put a bowl of bubble soap next to the first player of each line. Give each player his own straw.

At the starting signal, the first player of a line dips into the bowl, blows a good-size bubble and walks as quickly to the other side as possible without his bubble breaking away from the straw. Should this happen, the player must return to the bowl and blow another bubble.

When a player reaches the line on the opposite side, he shakes his bubble away from the straw. This signals the second player on the team to dip into the soap, blow a bubble, and cross the floor to the third player, and so on. The trick to the game is learning to blow a bubble that's just the right size. Too large a bubble will easily break away from the straw; too small a bubble will cling to the straw and be difficult to shake off when the player reaches the other side.

The first team to completely switch sides wins the game.

Cape in the Mud

Players: 4 or more in pairs
Materials: 4 towels of the same size for
  each team

Sir Walter Raleigh, the English nobleman, impressed Queen Elizabeth by throwing his cape over a muddy pool so that the Queen could step across. In this race, you'll do the same for your partner.

Mark starting and finish lines with books placed on opposite sides of the room or backyard. Players pair up and stand behind the start line. One player of each pair holds the two towels and is Sir Walter, the other player is the Queen.

At the start signal, each Walter throws a towel in front of his Queen. She steps on the towel and waits for him to throw the second towel. He does, she steps, and the Walters pick up their first towels to throw down again. The

race proceeds this way, in stepping-stone fash-
ion, until one pair of players reaches the finish
line and wins.

Chase the Caboose

Players: 10 or more in two teams
Materials: Chairs for each player

Arrange the chairs in two rows, facing each other. Each team takes a row.

At the signal, the first player of each team

gets up from his chair, races around the row of chairs, and takes his seat again. As soon as he's seated, the second player gets up and races around the row. The third player follows, then the fourth, until the last player of a team takes his seat.

Now the first player gets up and races again, but as soon as he passes the second player, she gets up and follows. As the second player passes the third player, he gets up and follows. The fourth player follows the third, and so forth, until the first team to get all of its players seated again wins the race.

Dictionary

Players: 3 or more
Materials: Dictionary, paper and pencil for
  each player

Players sit in a circle or around a table, each
with pencil and paper. The IT player opens the
dictionary and chooses a word, saying it aloud
to the other players. The word should be weird
and funny-sounding and not familiar to any of
the other players.

Each player makes up a definition for the
word and writes it down, hiding the paper from
neighbors. The definition should sound as real-
istic as possible so that it will fool the other
players. Only the IT player knows the real definition of the chosen word and writes it down.

All the players fold their papers and pass
them to the IT player. The IT player numbers
all the definitions and then, one by one, reads

them to the other players. Each player, except IT, must now choose the "correct" definition, and IT records the number chosen by each.

The player whose definition fools the most players gets a point for each player who chooses it. If a player chooses the correct definition, then the IT player gets a point. The player with the highest point score gets to be IT for the next round. Whoever has the most points after 10 rounds wins the game.

Don't Touch the Queen

Players: 7 or more
Materials: Chair

Choose one player to be the Queen. The Queen sits on the throne while another player stands next to her, guarding. The remaining players arrange themselves in a circle surrounding the Queen and her Guard.

Players run from the circle toward the Queen and try to tag her on the knee, shoulder, arm, or wherever they can reach. The Guard protects the Queen by running around the Queen and tagging the approaching players, but he must keep one hand on the Queen's throne at all times.

If too many players approach at once (usually more than three), the Queen can yell "Halt!" and all players must return to the circle. Then, before the game continues, the Queen may exact

a punishment by forcing the circled players to move 3 feet (1 m) away from her.

Any player who succeeds at touching the Queen takes the place of the Queen's Guard for the next round.

Doughnut Nose

Players: 8 or more in two teams

Materials: Box of small doughnuts (powdered sugar or cinnamon-sugar coatings
work best), plastic straw for each player

Teams line up single file, and each team member holds a straw. The first players in line
have the doughnuts. Each first player puts a

straw in his mouth and places the doughnut on the straw so that it slides down and hits his nose. This is the only time a player may use his hands.

At the start signal, the first player turns to the player in back of him and passes the doughnut to that player's straw. In turn, that player passes the doughnut to the player standing behind, and so on, until the last in line has the doughnut. That player rushes to the front of the line and starts the doughnut passing all over again.

If a player drops the doughnut, he must pick it up without using hands. And if a doughnut crumbles because of too much poking, a player can call "Time!" and replace his doughnut with a fresh one.

When the original doughnut passer gets to the front of the line again, he wins the race for his team. The player with the most powdered sugar or the most cinnamon smudge on his nose gets the booby prize.

Fruit Salad

Players: 6 or more
Materials: Chairs for each player, minus one

This game resembles Musical Chairs, except that no player gets eliminated by losing his seat. Choose one player to be IT, who stands. The rest of the players sit in a circle around him. Each of the sitting players chooses a fruit such as an orange, lemon, banana, grape, pineapple, or strawberry.

The game begins with IT calling out a pair of fruits, such as "bananas and strawberries!" Then, the banana and strawberry players must jump from their chairs and exchange places—if IT doesn't get to one of the chairs first. When that happens, the chairless player becomes IT, and IT takes the name of the fruit he replaced.

The real fun comes when IT calls out, "Fruit salad!" and all of the players rush to

exchange places. Whoever is left out becomes
IT for the next round, and the game continues
until everyone gets tired of playing.

Going to Texas

Players: 5 or more; Leader
Materials: None

This memory game has you saying the weirdest things. If memorizing isn't hard enough already, try doing it while you're laughing.

Players stand in a circle surrounding the Leader. The Leader announces that everyone is going to Texas and that each player can take along one thing. He turns to the first in the circle and asks her what she'll take. She might reply with, "I'll take my cowgirl hat." Then he asks the second player, who might say "I'll take my dog," then maybe the third player adds, "I'll take a peanut-butter sandwich."

After everyone in the circle states what they'll take to Texas, the Leader turns back to the first player and asks her what she'll do with her cowgirl hat. She has to reply in a complete sentence and say, "I'll wear my cowgirl hat in Texas." The Leader turns to the second player who must now say, "I'll wear my dog in Texas," and then to the third player, who says "I'll wear a peanut-butter sandwich in Texas."

This continues the second time around the entire circle, with each player "wearing" the article he chose earlier.

For the third time around the circle, the Leader asks the second player what he'll do with his dog in Texas. The player again replies with a complete sentence, "I'll scratch my dog in Texas"; the next player says, "I'll scratch my peanut-butter sandwich in Texas," and so on. The fourth time around the circle will begin with, "I'll eat my peanut-butter sandwich in Texas," and continue until the Leader goes around once for every player.

You'll find that sometimes the action fits the articles perfectly, although most of the time you'll get strange and funny combinations of things.

Grab the Gorilla

Players: 2; referee

Materials: Large table, blindfolds for each player

Although this game is best played with only two, your friends will enjoy watching it. Toss a coin to see which of the players becomes the Gorilla. The other player is the Hunter.

Blindfold the Gorilla and Hunter, and place them at opposite ends of a large table. At a signal from the referee, the Hunter tries to "catch" the Gorilla by grabbing him and holding on for 3 seconds. Of course, he can't see the Gorilla, and so stumbles around. The Gorilla, in turn, tries to keep away from the Hunter, but he doesn't know the Hunter's whereabouts.

Each tries to fool the other by giving false signals. The Hunter may tiptoe to one end of

the table and start pounding and then quickly run to the other end because he expects the Gorilla to run away from the noise. The Hunter may also whisper, call out, and give all kinds of misleading signals. The Gorilla may also make sounds and then run to a different spot to fool the Hunter.

Your friends will have a great time watching. Make sure they don't call out any clues to the Hunter or Gorilla. The only person who can speak is the referee, and only to warn the Hunter or Gorilla about crashing into something.

When the Hunter catches the Gorilla, the Hunter can either choose a new Gorilla from among the onlookers, or choose to have the Gorilla become the Hunter and do all the chasing in the next game.

Grandma Doesn't Like It

Players: 6 or more; Leader
Materials: None

The Leader announces, "My grandma doesn't like tea, but she likes coffee." This goes to each player standing in a line, and each replies with "Your grandma doesn't like tea, but she likes . . . ," substituting some other word for coffee.

However, there's a trick, and only the Leader knows it—at first. Let's say the game goes this way:

Leader: "My grandma doesn't like tea, but she likes coffee."

Player #1:   "Your grandma doesn't like tea. Does she like hot chocolate?"

Leader: "No, she doesn't like that."

Player #1:   "Does she like cherry tarts?"

Leader: "No, she doesn't like that."

Player #1: "Does she like roast turkey?"
Leader: "No, she doesn't like that!"
Player #1: "Does she like cookies?"
Leader: "Yes, she likes that."
Player #1: "Does she like apples?"
Leader: "Yes, she likes that. Do you understand what Grandma likes?"
Player #1: "Yes!"

If Player #1 "gets it," that is—if he figures out after two tries that Grandma doesn't like any food with the letter *T* in it, then he changes places with the Leader and goes through the routine with the next in line. If he doesn't catch on, the Leader continues to the next player in line.

You can change this game by substituting any secret "rule" that makes Grandma not like something. It doesn't have to be food. It could be, for example, that she dislikes any animal that flies, any flower with thorns, or any song with *kiss* in the words.

Eventually, all players figure out the trick, and the game becomes a challenge to see who can come up with the most clever things Grandma doesn't like!

Hats On, Hats Off

Players: 6 or more; referee

Materials: Round table; chairs for each player; hats for each player minus one; music (optional)

In this game, having a good time means grabbing your hat and sticking around. You can play it with musical accompaniment or have the referee chant out a tune or create a rhythm. The fun works either way.

Except for the referee, players sit around the table. Every player, except for IT, has a hat on his head. You can choose any style of hat for this game. Ski hats work well, but whatever you choose, make sure it's a hat that can slip on and off easily and doesn't mind getting a little roughed up.

The referee begins to chant, in rhythm, "Hats off . . . ," followed by a clap. All players

obey, removing their hats, tossing them in the center of the table, and clapping once. The referee continues, "Hats on . . . ," followed by another clap. All players pick up a hat (it doesn't have to be the original hat) and put it on. The IT player sits and watches.

The routine continues for a while, according to the referee's calls. If you use music, the referee makes his calls over the beat of the music.

At some point after hats are placed on the table, either before or after the clap, the referee shouts, "No hats!" If there's music, at this point, the music stops. Now players, including IT, have to grab for a hat. The player left without a hat goes out of the game, and one hat is removed.

The game continues until it's down to only two players, one of whom gets the last hat and wins.

Human Bingo

Players: 16 or more; Leader
Materials: Shoebox; paper and pencil for each player

Choose a Leader to do the Bingo calling. For the remaining players, divide a sheet of square paper into 16 squares. This means that each paper will have four squares to a side.

Players pass their sheets around so that every player initials every other player's sheet in one of the smaller squares. Each player should choose to initial a different square for each sheet. This ensures that no two players' sheets are the same.

Players write their names on another sheet of paper and the Leader cuts the names out and mixes them in a shoebox. He then pulls out one name at a time and announces it. The named player stands up and turns around

once, but doesn't mark his sheet. The remaining players mark their sheets over the named player's initials.

The first player to mark a complete row of initialed squares—horizontally, vertically, or diagonally—calls "Bingo!" and wins the game. He names the players of his row and they stand up and applaud him. Or they can tease him. Or they can force him to clean their rooms. You choose.

I Found the Cat

Players: 6 or more
Materials: Chairs for each player, two small
  objects

This game is a super memory-tester. Players
sit in a circle, close to each other. For the
objects, choose two dissimilar things that you
can easily pass around—an orange and a
banana, for example, or a book and a sponge.

Player #1 holds the two objects. He turns to
Player #2 on his right, and, holding the apple,
says: "I found the cat." He hands the apple
over. Player #2, holding the apple, replies, "The
what?" and Player #1 repeats, "The cat." Then
Player #2 turns to Player #3 to his right and
says, "I found the cat," handing over the apple.
Player #3 asks "The what?" and Player #2
repeats "The what?" to Player #1, who replies
once again, "The cat!" Player #2 then repeats

"The cat!" to Player #3, who now hands the apple to Player #4.

So this is how it works as Player #3 turns to Player #4 with the apple:

Player #3 (to #4):   "I found the cat."
Player #4 (to #3):   "The what?"
Player #3 (to #2):   "The what?"

Player #2 (to #1):	"The what?"
Player #1 (to #2):	"The cat!"
Player #2 (to #3):	"The cat!"
Player #3 (to #4):	"The cat!"

If all of that sounds pretty easy, hold on. Remember, Player #1 also has the banana. A minute or so after passing the cat, he turns to the player on his left, and, holding the banana, says, "I found the dog." You can guess the rest. Soon the room is filled with a chorus of dogs and cats.

Things get really scary when the two objects pass somewhere in the middle of the circle and both sets of questions and directions must get passed back to Player #1. If you're serious about the game, you can appoint a referee who listens for any slip-ups and eliminates the confused player. Otherwise, just play I Found the Cat for fun.

I Went to the City

Players: 6 or more; Leader
Materials: Chairs for each player

With the players seated in a circle, the Leader says "I went to the city." Player #2 asks, "What did you buy?" "A pair of shoes," the Leader replies, beginning to move his feet slightly—a movement that Player #2 must pick up and continue, along with Player #1, through the game.

Player #2 turns to Player #3 and says, "I went to the city." Player #3 asks, "What did you buy?" and Player #2 responds with, "A pair of shoes and a new hat," tapping his head while moving his feet. Player #3 must imitate the action while she turns to Player #4 and says, "I went to the city," adding a new article to the list along with a new motion.

The list and motions become longer and

longer until the last player in the circle has
quite a bit to remember. No one wants to be
last in this game. So as a variation, players can
abandon rotation and call out to any other
numbered player in the circle. Without any
player knowing if he'll be last, the suspense
and excitement of the game grows.

Knight of the Whistle

Players: 6 or more

Materials: Small plastic whistle, 1-foot (30-cm) piece of string, safety pin

This game really is all about playing a trick on one unsuspecting player, the Knight of the Whistle. To set up the trick, tie one end of the

string to the whistle and the opposite end to the safety pin. One of the players hides the whistle, string, and pin in her pocket.

Tell the Knight that he has to go through a very important ceremony of knighthood after which his skills will be tested. He must kneel down in front of one of the other players with his head almost touching the floor. While he does this, the remaining players surround him, pat his back, and recite four times, "Here is the Knight of the Whistle!"

During the patting, the player with the whistle quickly (but carefully) pins it to the Knight's back between the shoulder blades. The players then instruct the Knight to rise. They surround him in a circle, and the test begins.

The players tell the Knight that his skills will be measured by how quickly he can nab the whistle away from the player who last used it. Spin the Knight slowly around. When he stops, the player facing his back should carefully take the whistle, blow it, and drop it so that when the Knight spins around, the whistle will follow.

Immediately, the second player facing the Knight's back blows the whistle and drops it, so that each time the Knight turns to catch the whistler, the whistle disappears.

Keep this up until you feel so sorry for the poor Knight of the Whistle that you reveal the secret of the game.

The Lawyer

Players: 10 or more, an even number;
   Lawyer
Materials: A chair for each player

The players sit in two rows facing each other, but far enough apart so that the Lawyer can walk between the rows. Each player should have a partner opposite him.

The game begins as the Lawyer, walking between the rows, turns to one of the seated players and asks a question. But instead of the questioned player answering, his partner sitting opposite him does. This is the general rule of the game: Whenever the Lawyer addresses any player, the player sitting opposite the questioned player answers.

The trick of the game is in how crafty the Lawyer can get at forcing the questioned player to answer directly. For example, the Lawyer might ask a question that the opposite player can't answer—a question that requires some information that only the questioned player knows. Or he might ask a simple question so quickly that the questioned player answers without thinking. Or the Lawyer might jump so quickly from player to player that certain players become confused and answer out of turn.

In any case, when a questioned player answers directly, both players in that pair go out of the game. The single pair of remaining players wins.

Left & Right Sack Pop

Players: 8 or more in two teams
Materials: 2 paper sacks (bags) for each
player

If you like noisy relay games, this will do perfectly. Ten players to a team stand single file

with a paper sack under each foot. At the start signal, the end player reaches down, picks up the sack under his left foot, blows it up, and pops it. Immediately, he tags the player in front of him, and that player follows the same routine.

As soon as the first player in line pops his sack, he reaches down to his *right* foot and repeats the procedure, tagging the player behind him. That player then pops the sack under his right foot, and so on, until the last player pops his right foot sack and wins the game for his team.

Metronome

Players: 4 or more in pairs; referee
Materials: None

Players pair up and stand back to back. The pairs should stand about 20 feet (6 m) from the referee and space themselves out evenly.

Each player of a pair starts out with his arms hanging loosely. The referee begins to count, slowly and steadily, from one to 25. At the number 10, players raise one arm straight out with the hand turned sideways. At the number 11, they drop the arm down again. Arms go up for 12, down for 13, and so on, keeping strict time with the referee's counting.

Each player in the pair should agree beforehand which arm to use for the duration of the game. If one player decides to use the left arm, his partner should use the right arm. It's also important that each player doesn't see his partner's arm going up and down.

Pairs of players will have no trouble keeping their arms swinging together while the referee counts. But when the referee reaches the number 25, he stops counting aloud and instructs the players to continue counting in their heads. It won't be long before the players in each pair, once swinging their arms in perfect unison, will begin to slip. Soon certain players of a pair will swing arms exactly opposite each other—all the while counting silently and suspecting they're perfectly together.

The fun part is watching how the pairs will move in and out of "synch," so that, eventually, arms will swing in perfect unison again. This falling in and out of phase is very familiar to scientists who study motion, sound, and light. When the referee reaches 100 in his silent count, he tells players to freeze. Whichever pair of players appears the most coordinated is declared the winner.

Newspaper Race

Players: 2 or more

Materials: 2 sheets of newpaper for each
player

In this race, two players can compete or you
can turn it into a relay between teams.

For the two-person version, have each racer stand behind some kind of mark or line, and
give each two large sheets of newspaper.
Explain that the racers can step only on the
sheets of newspaper. This means that each racer must put down one sheet for the first foot,
put down another sheet for the second foot, and
then lift each sheet to start again. Any racer
stepping off the newspaper gets disqualified.
This is also true if one of the racers tears his
newspaper.

For the relay version, you'll need an equal
number of players on each team, and each

team should be evenly split between opposite ends of the racing course. Provide a stack of newpapers at both ends. When a player reaches the end, he has to crumple up his newpaper sheets, reach into the stack, and hand fresh sheets to the next racer. The first team to completely switch sides wins.

Noah's Ark

Players: 8 or more
Materials: None

In this game you can rely on a little help from
your teammates. Choose two leaders from
among the players. The rest of the players
break into two teams and stand in facing rows.
The leaders stand in front of their teams.

Toss a coin to decide which leader begins
the game. That leader, Leader #1, mentions an
animal beginning with the letter *A*. He then
slowly counts to 10, during which time the other leader, Leader #2, must name an animal
beginning with *A*. If she does, she immediately
follows with an animal beginning with *B* and
counts. During this time, Leader #1 comes up
with a *B* animal and follows with a *C* animal.
This naming of animals proceeds through the
alphabet, going back and forth between leaders.

The teams help their leaders by calling out the names of different animals. If a leader can't think of an animal name, even with the help of his teammates, the opposing leader can pull away one member of that team and add the player to his own team.

The letter X complicates things. The leader who has successfully named a W animal and must now move on to X calls "List!" She counts to 10 while the other leader lists as many animals as he can. The opposing team listens and keeps count. Then the sides reverse, with Leader #1 listing and the opposite team counting.

When the leaders reach the end of the alphabet, each leader takes the number of animals he listed and deducts the number of players he lost to the other team. If no players were lost, then the list number stands as is.

The team with the higher score wins the game.

Ocean Wave

Players: 12 or more
Materials: None

This fast-moving variation on Musical Chairs will have you bouncing all over the place. Players seat themselves in a circle leaving one

empty chair. One player, the Caller, stands in the center. Another player, IT, stands beside him. The caller suddenly yells, "Slide left!" or "Slide right!" and all the sitting players have to slide in the called direction to fill the empty chair.

When this happens, IT races for the nearest empty chair, but since all of the players slide at once, the location of the empty chair constantly changes. The Caller further complicates things by changing the direction of the slide again.

If IT finally gets himself an empty chair, that means another player loses a chair. The chairless player becomes IT for the next round.

Pass the Sponge

Players: 8 or more
Materials: Large sponge, chairs for all
  but 2 players

Except for two, players sit in a circle facing the center. A seated player holds the sponge. There are two standing players, one inside the circle and one outside.

Players seated in a circle begin passing the sponge. The sponge can move quickly or slowly, backward or forward, and it does not have to make a complete circle before reversing direction. Seated players can also pass the sponge above their heads or close to their feet—anything goes, with the exception that no seated player may stand.

At the same time, the inside player moves around the circle and tries to snatch the sponge from one of the seated players. If he manages to

get it, he must then toss it over the heads of the seated players to the outside player. Of course, his toss may be intercepted by any seated player, in which case the sponge gets passed around again and the chase continues.

If the inside player snatches the sponge and manages to pass it to the outside player, then the seated player who lost the sponge takes the place of the center player for the next round of the game.

Pebble Tag

Players: 6 or more

Materials: Pebble or any small object easily hidden in the palm

This is a tag variation of Who's Got the Button? Before you begin, select a safety zone for the running player. The safety zone can be a far wall, a chair, or any stable and stationary object, like a tree.

Select one player as IT. The rest of the players form a wide circle around IT, spacing themselves evenly. Each circle player holds his hands out in front of him, palms together.

IT walks around the inside of the circle, placing her hand between the palms of each player. She pretends to place a pebble in each player's hands, although only one player gets the real pebble. Each player pretends to be the pebble-keeper to heighten the suspense of the game.

Suddenly the player with the real pebble breaks away from the circle and runs to touch the safety zone. If he's tagged by anyone, he becomes IT for the next round. If he escapes, the game repeats with the original IT.

Pick a Peach

Players: 5 or more
Materials: None

Players form a line, single file. Each player has his hands on the shoulders of the player in front of him. The first player in the line becomes the Gardener. The last player is the Peach. One other player, the Customer, stands apart.

The Customer approaches the Gardener and says, "I'd like to buy a peach, please." The Gardener answers with, "I have a very nice one on the last tree of the row." The Customer can reply with, "Is it fuzzy or smooth? Pale or pink?" or use any other funny pretended description of the person at the back of the line. Of course, the Gardener answers with his own description, hopefully to the delight of everyone.

When the Gardener tells the Customer, "Get it!" this becomes the signal for the Peach

to break away from the back of the line and race to the front without getting tagged by the Customer. If the Peach makes it to the front of the line, the Customer starts all over with a new Gardener (the Peach) and a new Peach. If the Peach gets tagged, he becomes the Customer for the next round.

Here's a hint for Customers: Pretend to run down one side of the line and then reverse direction and run down the other side. You'll run right into the Peach!

Pillow Walk

Players: 4 or more

Materials: Blindfold, small pillows in different colors for each player

Blindfold one player and place him at the center of a circle. Tell the player that he has to

stand perfectly still with his feet apart so that the remaining players can gently toss their pillows between his legs.

At the count of three, the circle players surprise the center player by throwing their pillows wherever they want to smack him quite deliberately. When the pillow tossing is finished, someone tells the center player to begin walking in any direction.

The object of the game is for the center player to step on a pillow belonging to one of the circled players. When this happens, the center player changes places with this player. Usually, the center player is particularly eager to step on the pillow that hit him the hardest. Then, it's time to get even!

Pinch-O

Players: 6 or more; Leader
Materials: 2 blankets or sheets

This game and the game Brother Bob come from the heyday of college fraternity pranks.

The Leader chooses two players who get down into crawling positions. He covers each player with a blanket. One of the covered players knows the trick and will help fool the other covered player.

The Leader explains that someone from among the surrounding players will pinch each of the covered players. After the player is pinched, he can lift the blanket and try to identify his pincher. But first he must say to the other covered player, "Brother, dear, someone pinched me near!" "Who pinched you, brother?" asks his partner, at which point the pinched

player can lift the blanket and look around the room for the guilty party.

Let's say Player #1 knows the trick. The Leader covers both players with blankets. Player #1 quietly comes out from under this blanket, pinches himself and cries, "Brother, dear, someone pinched me near!" Player #2 asks, "Who pinched you, brother?" Player #1 pretends to guess and discover the guilty pincher.

Then Player #1 pinches Player #2. While Player #2 says, "Brother, dear, someone

pinched me near!" Player #1 crawls back under his blanket and asks, "Who pinched you, brother?" Player #2 raises the blanket, looks at all those surrounding him, and starts guessing. Of course, he's wrong each time—until he figures it out.

Pippity-Pop

Players: 6 or more
Materials: None

You'll need good ears and a quick mind for this word game that's a relative of Simon Says.

Choose one player for IT. The rest of the players stand in a row facing IT, who walks back and forth watching the players. Suddenly IT points his finger at one of the players and says either "Pippity-pop!" or "Poppity-pip!" The player singled out must respond quickly according to what she hears. For example, if she hears IT say "Pippity—" she must respond with "Pip!" before IT can say "Pop!" If she hears "Poppity—" she must say "Pop!" If IT completes his word before the player can respond, he trades places with the player. Or, in an elimination competition, he can choose to take the player out of the game.

For variety, especially when the game is down to just a few very good players, IT can choose to change the order of the response. For example, he may require that players answer "Pop!" to "Pippity!" and "Pip!" to "Poppity!" Getting tongue-tied is just part of the fun in this game.

Portrait of Uncle Bumby-Bump

Players: 4 or more; Judge

Materials: Large poster board, felt-tip marker, construction paper, scissors, transparent tape, blindfold

With the felt-tip marker, draw a large circle on the poster board, and attach it to a wall. This is the head of Uncle Bumby-Bump. On pieces of construction paper, draw and cut out the following: two eyes, nose, mouth, ears, mustache, beard, eyebrows, hair, and bow tie.

This is the face of Uncle Bumby-Bump that a blindfolded player will try to put together. Place a small piece of cellophane tape on each of the pieces and lay them out so that the other players can hand them, one at a time, to the blindfolded player.

The blindfolded player should stand about

6 feet (2 m) from the head of Uncle Bumby-
Bump. Spin the player around five times, and
hand her one of the eyes. Tell her that she now

has to make a portrait of Uncle Bumby-Bump and that the best portrait wins a prize.

Guide the player toward the head and let her place the eye where she thinks it should go. Then guide her back and give her the other eye. When she returns, give her the nose, and so forth, until the portrait is finished. Remove the blindfold and let her look at her work.

Before the next player is blindfolded, the judge studies the portrait and rates it on a scale of 1–10. The more closely it resembles a face, the higher the score. Then carefully peel the features of the face away and blindfold the next player.

When all the players have had a chance to make their portraits, the judge pronounces the winner. As an added surprise, the reward can be a kiss from Uncle Bumby-Bump—somebody you've dressed up in the next room who suddenly comes out and surprises everybody.

Pull Away

Players: 10 or more
Materials: None

This game tests both your strength and concentration. Players link elbows and stand in a circle. One player in the circle becomes the Leader who calls out the commands. Her first command is "Pull away!" and all players back up while keeping their elbows linked, making the circle very tight.

Players pull back as hard as they can and hold it until two players break the circle. Those players go out of the game and the circle reforms. If one of the eliminated players is the Leader who called out commands, the first player to the right of the caller becomes the new Leader.

After the now smaller circle re-forms, the Leader yells "Pull away!" again and the circle tightens. Or, the Leader can first command the players to come together. This means that everyone walks forward and scrunches together before the next pull-away command. Again, the two players who break the circle go out, and so on, until the last remaining pair of players win the game.

A variation of this game involves a Tickler who goes around the circle and tickles pairs of players as they pull away.

Right Is Wrong

Players: 2
Materials: None

Begin by standing opposite your friend. Tell him that no matter how smart he thinks he is, he won't be able to imitate seven simple gestures you make. Ask him to watch carefully as you demonstrate the gestures.

Begin by holding your left arm in front of you with your finger pointing out. Then turn your arm so that your finger points to your face. Draw an imaginary circle around your face and say, "The earth is round." Then point to each of your eyes and say, "Two eyes." Point to your nose and say, "Nose," and point to your mouth and say, "Mouth."

Challenge your friend to repeat the routine exactly. Unless your friend is left-handed, he'll almost certainly go through the routine using

his right hand, allowing you to say, "Wrong!"
and you can challenge him to try again.

If he still doesn't get it after the first few
attempts, tell him that you'll repeat the seven
gestures and ask him to watch very closely.
This time, do the gestures with your right
hand instead of your left. Now your friend will
probably try to imitate you using his left hand,
and, as he fumbles, discover the trick.

The Secret Key

Players: 6 or more

Materials: Key or other small object easily
   hidden in the palm of the hand

Choose one player as IT, and have the
remaining players form a circle around him.
The players in a circle hold hands in a strange
way. Instead of actually joining hands, each
player holds the wrist of the player to his left,
leaving the hand free. Joined together this
way, each player must be able to move his
right hand over to the left hand of his neighbor, as if passing something, so that all the
players in the circle can appear to make one
movement together.

Since all the players in the circle seem to
be passing something, the IT player will have
a hard time discovering the secret key as the
object moves from player to player. To begin,

IT closes his eyes so that he won't see who gets the key first, then opens them as the key starts to move. Circle players can try to distract the IT player by pretending to stumble with the key.

When the IT player thinks he sees the key, he touches the player he believes has it. If he's correct, he switches places with that player. If not, the game continues until he discovers the secret key.

Slippery Soap Relay

Players: 8 or more in two teams; referee
Materials: 2 bars of soap, 2 pans of water

This relay race will keep you laughing, but for the sake of neatness and safety, you should only do it on a noncarpeted surface, wearing nonslip shoes.

Measure 15 feet (4.5 m) for each of the courses. You can use a chair, book, or some other object to mark the beginning and end of each course. It doesn't matter which end you choose for starting, but both teams should agree. At the starting ends, place bowls of water and drop bars of soap in the bowls. Let the soap get good and slimy.

Divide your team in half so that an equal number of players stand at opposite ends of the course. The first player of each team stands beside his bowl. His teammates line up behind

him and stand in a line at the opposite end of the course, waiting.

At a signal from the referee, Player #1 of each team reaches into the bowl with one hand, grabs the soap bar, and runs across to Player #2. Using only *one hand*, Player #2 must take the slippery soap from Player #1 and race across to Player #3. If any of the players drops his slippery soap, he must stop to pick it up, with one hand only, then go back to the beginning of the course.

The first team to completely switch sides wins the race.

Sloppy Cereal Race

Players: 4 or more in pairs
Materials: String; breakfast cereal; milk;
bowl and tablespoon (or large spoon) for
each player

It takes both speed and coordination to win
this race. Prepare for it by tying 2 tablespoons
together with a 6-inch (15-cm) length of string.

Make a set of these tied spoons for each pair of players. Place a bowl on the table for each player, and measure out 2 cups (480 ml) of cereal per bowl. You can leave out the milk if you want, but adding milk makes this race good and sloppy, as promised.

Pairs of players sit at their bowls and pick up their spoons. At the signal, each player dives into his cereal and eats, while trying not to pull the spoon away from his teammate. It gets very sloppy, but the first pair of players to finish wins the race. As a reward, you can untie their spoons and give them a fresh bowl of cereal.

Spell Down

Players: 6 or more
Materials: None

This game adds an unusual twist to the spelling bee in that the player who actually spells a word correctly has to moo like a cow!

The first in a circle of players chooses a letter that's part of a word he has in mind. The next player chooses another letter, and the following player chooses yet another letter, the object being that each player must add a letter but avoid completely spelling a word. The first player who spells a word or runs out of letters is taken out of the game and has to moo like a cow while the others continue to play.

A player who adds a letter must always have a word in mind, and any player who appears to buy time with nonsense letters can be challenged by any of the others in the circle. If, when challenged, the player cannot produce a word, then he is taken out of the game and must moo. If the challenged player produces a word, then the challenger is taken out and must moo. By elimination, the last remaining player wins the game.

Spoons

Players: 2 or more; referee
Materials: Teaspoon or small spoon

You can play spoons as a match between two
players, teams, or with several players competing by elimination and rematch. Whichever
way you choose, this simple game is still a
favorite.

Two players sit on the floor facing each other. The referee places a teaspoon between them at a distance of no more than arm's length for each player. Players clasp their hands behind their backs—the referee should make sure of this.

At the signal, each player whips a out a hand and tries to snatch the spoon from the floor before his opponent can reach it. It doesn't matter which hand a player chooses, but once a spoon is picked up, the losing player can't grab it. The snatched spoon goes behind the winner's back for 1 point. The first player to accumulate 10 points wins the game.

As a variation, the referee can place six spoons between the players. Players are therefore challenged to be strong as well as quick. A player who darts for spoons but picks up only two, while his slower, more calculating opponent gets the remaining four, will be at a disadvantage. With this variation, the first player to reach 50 points wins the match.

Squirrel Tails

Players: 6 or more in two teams; referee

Materials: Bag of peanuts; masking tape;
belt for each player; strip of cloth for each
player, with a different color for each team

Tie a strip of cloth onto the belt of each player
and divide the players into two teams. With
masking tape, mark out two safety lines at
opposite sides of the room. Teams stand behind
these lines, facing each other.

The referee places several handfuls of
peanuts in the center of the room, and at the
signal, all the Squirrels rush to the center of
the room and pick up as many peanuts as they
can. Squirrels from opposing teams try to pull
each others' "tails." When a Squirrel gets his
tail pulled, he goes out of the game and his
peanut treasure is lost. The puller also gets 5
points for taking a Squirrel out.

Squirrels try to run back across their safety lines without getting their tails pulled. At the end of the game, the referee counts the peanuts each team has, and along with the point total for eliminated players, declares one team the winner.

Stair-Step Spelling

Players: 5 or fewer, depending on width of
  stairs

Materials: Dictionary

This variation of the old-fashioned spelling bee has the winner on top. Choose one player, the Reader, to select words at random from the dictionary. The remaining players stand at the top of a flight of stairs—the more stairs, the better.

The Reader chooses the first word and calls it to Player #1. If Player #1 spells the word correctly, he stays put. Then Player #2 gets a word. If she spells it correctly, she remains at the top of the stairs with Player #1. But if she misspells the word, she must go down one step. Player #3 gets a word and follows the same rules. Any player who, after having stepped down, spells correctly on the next turn, gets to step up again. But a player who keeps misspelling words steps

down for each mistake until he steps off the stairs completely and goes out of the game.

You can play the game two ways, either by allowing it to continue for only a certain amount of time, at the end of which the highest player is declared the winner. Or, you can play until only one player remains on the stairs while all the others have stepped off.

Stand & Pop

Players: 10 or more in two teams
Materials: Paper bag for each player

This relay type of game is guaranteed to keep things popping. Prepare by passing out a paper bag to each player. Small lunch bags work pretty well.

Players divide into two teams, three teams if you have lots of players. The players of each team stand single file and about 2 feet (60 cm) from each other. Each player holds an unopened paper bag.

At the start signal, the players at the end of each line quickly blow up their bags and pop them on the backs of the players in front of them. This signals the players in front to pop their bags on the backs of the players in front of *them*. The routine continues until the first player in a line blows up his bag and pops it on his knee, winning the game for his team.

Stand & Stoop

Players: 5 or more; Leader
Materials: None

In this variation of Simon Says, words and actions go their separate ways. Players of Stand and Stoop will have as much fun leading or following.

The players stand beside one another in the line facing the Leader. The Leader shouts, "I say stoop!" and all the players follow his example. He then says, "I say stand!" and all the players stand. Sound simple? Not when the Leader increases his speed so that players stoop and stand so fast that they hardly have time to think. A command must always begin with "I say." Any player who obeys the simple command "stand!" or "stoop!" goes out of the game.

To further complicate the challenge, the

Leader can say one thing and do another. For example, if he says, "I say stoop" while in a stoop, and fools some players into standing, those players go out. So not only must players listen carefully, but they have to watch the Leader's every move.

The one remaining player at the end of the game is declared the winner and switches places with the Leader for the next game.

Statues

Players: 6 or more
Materials: None

All players stand in a line except one. The lone
player stands about 15 feet (4.5 m) away with
her back to the line, and covers her eyes. Then

she slowly and silently counts to 10. While she counts, the players in line creep across the room to reach the other side. When the counting player spins around and opens her eyes, creeping players must freeze like statues in whatever position they're in. Any player caught midcreep, or who begins to move while frozen, gets sent back to the beginning.

Players who can take long, quiet strides across the room have the best chance of beating their friends. However, these strides are usually the hardest to freeze and keep without tumbling over. The counting player can take as long as she wants to study the frozen players before counting again.

The first player to make it to the other side becomes the counter in the next game.

Still Pond

Players: 5 or more
Materials: Blindfold

Choose one player as IT and blindfold him. The other players surround him. One of the players asks, "How many fish in the pond?" IT answers by giving the number of players surrounding him. The player then says, "Count them out," at which point IT spins around once for every player.

While IT spins, the circle players creep away—no running allowed. They freeze when IT finishes his spin and calls out "Still pond!" IT might be a little dizzy by the time he calls, depending on how fast he spun around. He can choose to spin slowly, in which case the players have more time to creep away, or he can spin quickly, giving the players less time but making himself woozier. Of course, if there are a lot

of players to count, he'll get dizzy either way!

After the players freeze, IT carefully moves toward any of them. Players should keep quiet and avoid laughing. As IT approaches a player, the player may take, only once, three steps in any direction to get away. A player may also bend around, crouch, or do whatever she needs to avoid getting touched, as long as she doesn't move from her position—assuming she's already taken her three steps.

A touched player must stand and allow IT to touch his face and hair. IT then tries to identify the player with one guess. If correct, the identified player and IT trade places for the next round. If incorrect, IT must move to another player.

Stormy Sea

Players: 8 or more in pairs
Materials: Chairs for each pair of players,
  minus two

Players pair up, sit down, and each pair chooses the name of a fish or another sea creature,
which they keep to themselves. Only one pair
of unseated players can identify themselves as
mammals, the Whales. The Whales walk
around the room calling out the names of fish.
The pair whose fish is named get up and follow
the Whales around the room. If several couples
have the identical fish name, then they follow
together.

The Whales can take their parade of fish
anywhere throughout the house or yard, and
pairs of players whose fish names are never
called can remain in their seats.

Suddenly, the Whales call out "Stormy

Sea!" and all players must rush back to the chairs and take seats next to their partners. If one member of a pair finds a seat, but her partner is seatless, both players must find other seats. The seated pairs can remain seated, of course, as a reward for having a rather unusual, unguessed, fish name.

Any pair left without seats become the Whales for the next round.

Swamp Monster

Players: 8 or more in two teams; Monster
Surface: Grassy or sandy (outdoors); carpeted floor (indoors)

Players get into teams, and the teams line up
facing each other across the Swamp. Instead of
standing, players kneel or crouch.

The Swamp is about 20 feet (6 m) of clear
space separating the teams. The Swamp
Monster lives in the Swamp and "swims"
(crawls) back and forth looking at each player.

The Monster chooses a player, points to
her, and then closes his eyes and slowly counts
aloud to 10. In turn, the chosen player must
point to a player on the opposite team. These
players must exchange places by crawling
through the Swamp as quickly as they can
without getting discovered by the Monster.
When the Monster opens his eyes, he crawls

after either of the players, and tries to tag one of them.

Here, you can either choose to have the tagged player go out, in which case the Swamp Monster remains for the rest of the game, or you can have the tagged player and Swamp Monster change places. Having the tagged player go out means that one team loses a player and that the surviving team will eventually win the game.

Tall & Small

Players: 5 or more; Leader
Materials: Blindfold

Players form a circle with one player in the middle, who's blindfolded. One player in the circle becomes the Leader and the rest follow her. She crouches, and along with the others says, "I am very, very small." Then she stands and says, "I am very, very tall." She repeats the crouch, saying, "Sometimes I'm small." Then she stands up again and says, "Sometimes I'm tall." For the next move, she can remain standing or crouch again, but says, "Which am I now?" The blindfolded player must guess from the sound of the voices around him.

This isn't as easy as it sounds. But for an even more difficult variation, have each member in the circle choose to crouch or stand, but independently of the others. Each will say he is tall or small depending on his position, and the sound of so many voices saying different things at the same time will challenge the blindfolded player. He circles and points to someone, who asks, "Which am I now?" From the sound of a single voice, the blindfolded player guesses.

If he's correct, he changes places with the called-out player. If not, he repeats the routine until he gets it right.

Tarp Ball

Players: 4; referee
Materials: Large sheet, large rubber ball

Each of the players takes a corner of the sheet with two hands. Then the players move away from one another so that the sheet stretches out between them. The referee places the ball in the center of the sheet.

At the signal, each player tries to lift a corner of the sheet so that the ball rolls toward one of the other players' corners. The object is to keep the ball from rolling into your corner and hitting one of your hands. If that happens, the player who rolled the ball toward you gets 1 point.

Since it isn't always easy to see who's scoring, the referee has to watch carefully.

The first player to accumulate 21 points wins the game.

Tied Balloon Race

Players: 14 or more in two teams
Materials: 4 balloons, 2 strips from an old
  sheet

This relay race requires just the right touch.
Prepare for the race by tearing two 2-foot (60-
cm) strips from an old sheet. Cut each 2-foot
(60-cm) strip in half and tie the halves together
so that each half can easily pull away from the
other. This requires a simple knot, shown in
the diagram. You should wind up with two 2-

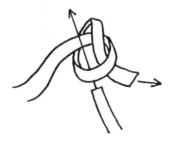

Here's the knot.

foot (60-cm) strips again, each tied together in the middle.

You should teach all the other players how to tie this knot before starting the game. Next, blow up four balloons, and tie the free ends of each strip to a balloon so that you have two pairs of tied balloons. Hand each team a pair of these tied balloons.

Players of each team stand side by side with about 2 feet (60 cm) of space between each player. The two teams stand back-to-back so that the first player of each team stands on an opposite side of the room. These players each hold a pair of tied balloons.

At the start signal, the first player passes one of the balloons to the next player, who passes it to the player after him. Since the balloons are connected, the first player must soon follow one balloon with the other, making sure that the first balloon hasn't gotten so far away that it will pull away from the second balloon.

As the balloons continue to move through the line, players must take care to pass the balloons quickly without pulling one balloon from the other. If this happens, the players must stop and reconnect the balloons before they can continue to pass them along. The first team to move its pair of balloons all the way down the line and back again wins the race.

Towel Ball

Players: 4 in two teams, referee
Materials: 2 beach towels, 2 stacks of books,
   medium-size rubber ball, yarn

This will remind you a little of volleyball, and
it can be just as challenging. Make the low
"net" by stretching out a piece of yarn the
width of your playing area. Keep the yarn off
the floor by placing it between stacks of books
at each end.

   Each team has two players who stand
stretching a beach towel between them on
opposite sides of the net. Teams will both catch
and toss the ball by using their stretched towels only.

   The referee begins the game by standing
beside the net and tossing the ball in the air.
Teams race with their towels to catch the ball,
and the first team that does, bounces the ball

out of its towel across the net to their opponents. Teams catch and toss their balls over the net until a team misses, scoring 1 point for the opposing team. A team can also score if the opposite team pitches the ball out-of-bounds (called by the referee), or hits the net with the ball. Any player who stumbles into the net also scores 1 point for the opponents.

The first team to reach 21 points wins the game.

Twos & Threes

Players: 12 or more
Materials: None

All but two players pair up, one behind the other, and stand in a circle so that an inner and outer circle are formed. Each pair of players should leave about 4 feet (1.3 m) of space between them. The remaining two players flip a coin to see who becomes IT and who gets chased around the circles.

IT takes his position outside the circles and the chased player stands inside the circles. At a signal, IT chases the other player by walking very fast (no running allowed), and each player weaves in and out of the two circles.

When the chased player gets tired of the chase, she gets herself inside the circles and stands in front of one of the pairs of players. Now the outside person of this pair becomes the chased player, and the game continues. If the chased player wants to trick IT, she walks to the outside circle and stands behind one of the players. Now the inside person becomes IT. The game keeps going until the chased player gets tagged by IT.

Umbrella Bounce

Players: 2 or more
Materials: Umbrella, large ball
Surface: Smooth

This tossing game requires a keen eye and just the right touch. Too much force will get you nowhere. Open the umbrella and turn it upside

down. If the umbrella has a point, it will probably roll around crazily—but that's fine.

The players stand about 10 feet (3 m) from the umbrella. The first player takes the ball and tosses it toward the bowl of the umbrella. It's not enough to just hit the umbrella, the ball must *stay* there for 1 point. If the player's ball rolls out, he retrieves it and hands it to the next player, who gets a turn. If the ball stays put, the player receives 1 point and gets to toss again. A successful player can continue tossing until his ball either misses or rolls out of the umbrella.

The first player to reach a score of 25 points wins the game.

In the unlikely event that the first player racks up 25 points at a single turn, the next player still gets his chance to do the same and tie the game.

Umbrella Roll Bowl

Players: 3 or more; referee
Materials: Umbrella, small rubber ball
Surface: Smooth

For this game, find an umbrella that has a good point at the end. The referee places the upside-down umbrella at the far side of the

room and stays with it. The other players stand about 15 feet (4.5 m) from the umbrella.

The game begins as the referee takes the umbrella handle and slowly rolls the umbrella around on its point. This means that only part of the umbrella's edge touches the floor and that part is constantly moving. The referee keeps rolling the umbrella for the entire game.

Each player must roll a ball toward the umbrella at precisely the moment when the umbrella's edge, the edge that faces them, touches the floor. If a player times it right, his ball will roll right into the umbrella and stay there for 1 point. If he miscalculates, the ball will either hit the edge of the umbrella, roll in and out again, or miss the umbrella completely. Players take turns as referee, rolling the umbrella. The first player to accumulate 21 points wins the game.

Unmentionables

Players: 4 or more
Materials: None

Two players secretly decide between them to discuss some object without mentioning the object by name. The idea is to both give hints and confuse the other players at the same time.

For example, if the object is a rose, the conversation might go something like this:

Player #1:   "I saw one in the yard yesterday."
Player #2:   "How big was it?"
Player #1:   "Enormous! And it smelled great!"
Player #2:   "Is it still there?"
Player #1:   "No, I took it inside and put it in water."
Player #2:   "I saw one too, but I'm afraid to touch it."
Player #1:   "You should always wear gloves."

As the other players listen to the conversation, one of them may think he knows the unmentionable object. This player raises his hand and calls, "Guess!" The conversation stops and the guessing player whispers into

the ear of the discussing players. If he's correct, he joins the conversation and attempts to confuse the remaining players. If he's wrong, he sits back and listens some more.

But the real fun of this game starts when more players wind up discussing than guessing. In fact, the one or two clueless players who still don't get it will start to feel pretty silly. Don't laugh too hard.

Who's Got the Button?

Players: 5 or more; referee

Materials: A button, coin, or any other small object you can hide in the palm of your hand

You can play this traditional American game with players standing in a circle or in a line.

Players stand with their hands cupped and held close to the body. The referee walks close to each player and pretends to put the button in each pair of cupped hands. Players in turn may pretend to receive the button. Of course, only one player gets the button, and it's up to the others to discover who he is. But since every player is potentially the Button Holder, and players get points for fooling their friends, some play-acting may be encouraged.

After the referee finishes his walk, he turns to the players and asks, "Who's got the button?" Player #1 answers by giving the name or number of some other player he suspects. Player #2 also identifies another player, and Player #3 follows suit. All players, including the one who actually has the button, identify another player as the guilty party. The referee keeps track of how many times each player is named.

After everyone has a chance to guess, the true Button Holder identifies himself. The referee awards each player—including the Button Holder—1 point for every accusation someone made against him. Only the Button Holder's accusations aren't counted.

Wiggums

Players: 6 or more
Materials: Potato, chair for each player

Players sit in a circle, facing center. One player holds the potato and starts the game by turning to the player on his right, introducing himself by name, and then introducing the potato.

For example, if Joe is the first player, he turns to Louise, the player on his right, and says, "Hi, I'm Joe." Then he hands Louise the potato and adds, "And this is Wiggums." Louise takes the potato, turns to Peter on her right, and says, "Hi, I'm Louise." She hands the potato to Peter, adding, "Joe says that this is Wiggums." When Peter passes the potato, he'll say, "Louise says that Joe says that this is Wiggums." The game continues with the list of names growing longer and always ending with Wiggums.

Obviously, the first few players have it easy. Any player who misses a name or says a name

out of order leaves the game, and his name drops from the list. This means that the circle gets smaller. But the potato Wiggums continues to go around, and if a player passes it twice, that player must be named twice by all the others.

The few remaining players will have to repeat each other's names many times as Wiggums goes around the shrinking circle. Players go out as they make mistakes, and the single remaining player wins the game.

Winders & Unwinders

Players: 4 in pairs; referee
Materials: 2 balls of yarn

This game is divided between the Winders and the Unwinders. One person in each pair plays the Unwinder and the other the Winder.

The game begins by having one player from each competing pair of players take the ball of yarn and unwind it for his opponents. For example, the Unwinder from Pair #1 takes the yarn from Pair #2 and unwinds it all over the room, making as complicated a path as possible. At the same time, the Unwinder from Pair #2 takes the yarn from Pair #1 and does the same. Players may unwind their opponents' ball of yarn only while the referee counts aloud to 20. After that, the Unwinders must stop wherever they are and return to their partners.

Now it's the Winders' turn. When the referee says "Go!" the Winders of each pair furiously
wind the yarn back into a ball. Neither one
may move from his position. The first Winder
to gather up all his yarn wins the game for
himself and his partner.

Wink & Tag

Players: 4 boy-girl pairs; single girl
Materials: 9 chairs, one for each person

Arrange the chairs in a circle so that each chair sits about 5 feet (1.5 m) from its neighbors. The boys sit in the chairs and the girls stand

behind them. The single girl stands behind an empty chair.

The single girl stares at each boy and each boy stares back. Suddenly, she gives one of the boys a big wink. That boy jumps from his chair and tries to run for the single girl's chair before the girl in back of him tags him. If he makes it, the girl who originally stood in back of him must now do the winking. If he's tagged, then the winking girl continues to wink until her chair is filled.

After a few rounds, the boys and girls trade places.

Index

347